HOW WALL STREET WORKS

THE BASICS AND BEYOND

DAVID L. SCOTT

IRWIN
Professional Publishing®
Chicago • London • Singapore

This publication is designed to provide accurate and authoritative information in regard to the subject matter covered. It is sold with the understanding that the publisher is not engaged in rendering legal, accounting, or other professional service.

ISBN 1-55738-267-0

Printed in the United States of America

BB

8 9 0

To the Vernon Moore family of Green Acres

CONTENTS

PREFACE

Many individuals view Wall Street as a murky world of great riches and even greater risks where greedy robber barons wait to pounce on neophyte investors. This view is not without justification because Wall Street does reward some of its players with impressive riches while at the same time other individuals lose substantial fortunes—often with great public fanfare. In large part, however, Wall Street is a collection of institutions that raise capital for private and public organizations that supply the kinds of investments that individual and institutional investors demand. The investments are sometimes very risky and subject investors to a real possibility of substantial losses. Other investment vehicles are as safe as certificates of deposit. For example, Wall Street continues to supply the world with one of its lowest-risk and least complicated investments—U.S. Treasury securities.

The goal of this book is to take much of the mystery out of investing by providing an overview of the complicated world of Wall Street. The following chapters describe the various organizations that comprise Wall Street along with the types of securities that Wall Street makes available. An emphasis is placed on a discussion of stocks and bonds and how these securities are traded on the organized exchanges. A chapter is also devoted to answering some of the most common questions concerning the New York Stock Exchange. Another chapter discusses some of the newer investments including put and call options, stock warrants, and convertible bonds. Wall Street has produced a great many new investment vehicles over the past ten to fifteen years.

There is a chapter devoted to the topic of how to open a brokerage account along with a look at the safety of the securities and cash that are kept in these accounts. You will learn how you may save on interest costs by borrowing money from a brokerage account. Have you wondered how to interpret the stock and bond tables that appear in the daily newspaper? Chapter Eight covers this topic.

Don't overlook the appendix material at the back of the book. Here you will find a glossary of Wall Street terms and a historical look at stock averages, interest rates, and inflation rates. The appendix also includes the names, addresses, and phone numbers of firms that you may need to contact. In short, this book is indeed intended to help you understand how Wall Street works.

David L. Scott
Valdosta, Georgia

Chapter 1

WHAT AND WHERE IS WALL STREET?

CHAPTER SUMMARY

Wall Street is a street in New York City; at the same time it represents a central market where securities are issued and traded. This chapter presents an introduction to Wall Street: how it assists America's capitalistic economy function more efficiently, who works there, how is it regulated, and how safe investors' money is. Most of the topics treated in this chapter will be discussed at greater length in later chapters.

What is Wall Street?

Wall Street is a place where businesses sell shares of ownership, where the United States Treasury routinely borrows billions of dollars to finance the federal deficit, where investors trade a variety of financial claims including stocks and bonds, and where financial services companies distribute mind-numbing amounts of financial information. Wall Street is a place where huge money-center banks make mega-sized loans, where frenzied traders in bright jackets with name tags dangling from their pockets shout orders to buy and sell stocks and bonds and a variety of other financial assets, and where powerful computers process the daily paperwork for hundreds of thousands of transactions.

Exactly what is a stock and what is a bond?

Stock represents ownership in a business concern. For example, Black and Decker Corporation, a manufacturer and marketer of power tools and small appliances, has outstanding 59 million shares of common stock. Each share represents a single ownership unit of Black and Decker. Because most of Black and Decker's owners have more than a single share of stock, there are only 21,000 different owners including 200 institutional investors that own approximately half the outstanding shares.

A bond represents a debt that is owed to the owner of the bond. Businesses, national governments, state governments, and municipalities borrow money by selling bonds. Bonds generally require the borrower to make periodic interest payments and to repay the amount borrowed on a specific date.

Is trading stocks and bonds the main activity on Wall Street?

The issuing and trading of stocks and bonds are two of Wall Street's major activities but are certainly not the only activities. The decade of the eighties witnessed the introduction of a whole host of new financial assets that are sold and traded by Wall Street organizations. Investment vehicles such as calls, puts, warrants, financial futures contracts, commodity contracts, and partnerships are only a few of the multitude of investments in which Wall Street deals. Any asset of a financial nature is likely to have at least some connection with Wall Street.

Is there any difference between the market in which financial assets are first sold and the financial market in which the assets are later traded?

Financial assets such as stocks and bonds are issued in the *primary market*, a part of Wall Street in which investors' funds flow to businesses and governments which issue financial claims (also called *securities*) that evidence the investments. Once financial claims have been issued, many of the securities continue to be traded among investors in the secondary market, which includes the stock exchanges. The same organizations that originally issued the financial assets in the primary market do not participate in trading the securities in the secondary market.

But don't the organizations that issue the securities need to keep track of the investors who own their securities?

Organizations do stay current on the owners of their securities. Otherwise, a company with publicly traded stock would not know who owned the firm and a government that had borrowed money would not know who was to receive the interest checks. Not participating in secondary market trading means that the issuers of stocks and bonds are not actively involved in buying, selling, or trading their own stocks and bonds once these securities have been issued.

Is the New York Stock Exchange part of the primary market or part of the secondary market?

Existing financial assets (e.g., securities that have already been issued) are traded on the New York Stock Exchange.

Thus, the exchange is part of the secondary market. All of the activity on the floor of the exchange involves investors trading stocks and bonds with other investors or with exchange members. The companies that originally issued the securities—the firms whose names are imprinted on the face of the certificates—are not represented on the exchange.

Is there a single street where all of these activities take place? Is there a real street named *Wall Street*?

Wall Street certainly does exist. It is located at the south end of Manhattan Island in downtown New York City. However, *Wall Street* is often spoken of in the sense that it is a marketplace encompassing all of the activities that are related to the issuance and trading in financial assets. For example, the term *Wall Street* is frequently used as a frame of reference to identify the major financial institutions and markets that are scattered all across the country.

In a more narrow sense, *Wall Street* refers to the major financial institutions and markets that are located in and around New York City. The more restrictive definition still includes financial institutions that are near but not directly on Wall Street as well as institutions that have a Wall Street address. In this sense, *Wall Street* is used in reference to financial markets as opposed to a particular location.

How did Wall Street grow from being a street in New York City to represent a major part of the entire U.S. financial system?

The financial system has experienced a major evolution, especially over the last several decades. At one time, nearly all major financial transactions either took place in or had some direct connection with New York City. Not surprisingly, the firms that were involved in conducting these transactions had a strong presence on Wall

Street. As population and wealth gradually shifted away from the Northeast toward the West and the South, and as computing and communications systems technology leapfrogged ahead, many of the functions that were once confined to the Wall Street area began to take place outside New York City. However, Wall Street has historically been the place where most major financial transactions originate and the term continues in use even though it often refers to similar activities that occur away from the old financial district.

Is Wall Street part of or somehow associated with the federal government?

Activities on Wall Street are heavily regulated by the federal government but most of the financial institutions that operate on Wall Street are privately owned and independently operated. These private concerns include commercial banks, stock exchanges, brokerage firms, and investment bankers. Wall Street prides itself on being the heart and soul of the free enterprise system, even though this system is subject to a substantial amount of direction from the federal government.

One of the major players on Wall Street is an important part of the federal government. The Federal Reserve Bank of New York is the branch of the Federal Reserve System that auctions Treasury securities and that implements the government's monetary policy. The actions of the Federal Reserve have an impact on interest rates, inflation rates, and security prices.

When did the "real" Wall Street commence operations?

Commodities such as tobacco and grains were traded at the foot of Wall Street as early as the early- to mid-1700s. In the late 1700s, a separate market developed for financial securities and Wall Street commenced trading Revolutionary War bonds and the stock of the First Bank of the United States. The first formal agreement among brokers for what was later to become the New York Stock Exchange was drawn up about this same time and the organization adopted the name *New York Stock and Exchange Board* in the early 1800s. By the mid-1800s, substantial trading was taking place in the stocks and bonds of transportation companies, especially railroads and canals. Industrial expansion following the Civil War brought a broader spectrum of securities to Wall Street.

Securities are now traded in many places other than New York City?

New York continues to be the financial hub of the United States and the home for two of the country's largest financial markets: the New York Stock Exchange and the American Stock Exchange. Similar, but smaller financial markets are located in Chicago, San Francisco, Los Angeles, Boston, and Philadelphia. A great variety and increasing number of financial assets are traded via computer and telephone rather than in a central location. Continuing improvements in computers and communications are likely to produce additional changes in the methods by which financial assets are traded. Many financial experts feel that the days are numbered for securities trading at a central physical location such as the New York Stock Exchange. These individual argue that improvements in communications have already made these marketplaces obsolete.

Does this mean that many of the activities associated with Wall Street will increasingly take place outside New York City?

It seems likely that financial activities once relegated solely to the New York area will occur more and more frequently in other locations. Some professionals foresee the day when security trades will occur from virtually any location. A computer linked with up-to-date quotations and other traders will permit an individual to perform the same activities at any location that now take place in New York City. Most of the technology for such a system is already available.

If the centralized markets such as the New York Stock Exchange are obsolete why do they continue in operation?

Critics contend that there are many wealthy individuals and important organizations with vested interests in keeping changes from occurring too rapidly. A great amount of money is invested in the existing financial marketplaces and it is not always in the interest of the people who have made these investments to see their importance diminished as competing markets gain status in financial transactions.

If I purchase stock through my local broker will the order end up in New York?

Your broker's firm may route the order to New York or it may send the order to some other location. Where your order is executed depends upon where the brokerage firm has its trading facilities and the location where your security is normally traded. For example, the order may be routed to San Francisco and executed on the Pacific Stock Exchange. If the financial asset is traded at several locations your brokerage firm should attempt to have the transaction executed where you will obtain the best price.

How important is Wall Street to the functioning of the U.S. economy?

Wall Street plays a major role in both the domestic and the international economies. Wall Street facilitates the accumulation of capital by private businesses which, in turn, allows these businesses to construct factories, manufacture equipment, supply services, and provide jobs to the country's citizens. Large and active securities markets make it easier for private businesses and governments to raise funds because individuals who invest in these organizations have confidence that the investments can later be sold to other investors without undue difficulty. Without Wall Street (or something akin to Wall Street), organizations would find it relatively cumbersome and more expensive to raise capital. Inefficient financial markets result in slower economic growth, less competitiveness on the part of domestic businesses, and fewer jobs for the country's citizens.

Are the fortunes of Wall Street dependent upon a healthy economy?

History has shown that a sick economy—inflation, rising unemployment, and recession—is generally accompanied by troubles on Wall Street. Investors who become apprehensive are likely to be more conservative in their investments so that Wall Street firms will find their own business deteriorating. A healthy economy is good medicine for Wall Street.

Do other countries have their own versions of "Wall Street?"

Developed countries that function with a capitalistic economy require some method of bringing together segments of the economy having excess capital with segments of the economy that desire additional capital for investment purposes. There are a number of financial centers around the world that provide this service, several with a size that rivals Wall Street. Keep in mind that foreign-based companies often use Wall Street to raise capital just as U.S.-based firms frequently use foreign markets for raising capital. Wall Street is becoming more and more a global concept as financial centers around the world are linked through telecommunications.

What types of employment are available on Wall Street?

Wall Street is the home to brokers, dealers, portfolio managers, investment advisors, specialists, bond traders, stock traders, and a whole host of other professionals who make their living in the business of buying, selling, and managing investments. Most of these job titles, which may be unfamiliar, will be discussed later in this book.

Do people who are employed on Wall Street make a lot of money?

As is the case with many other occupations, some individuals on Wall Street do very well while other individuals barely make enough income to get by. Also, income earned by brokers, traders, and investment managers is subject to substantial variation from one year to the next. Some brokers and investment managers have been on top of the world with income in the hundreds of thousands of dollars one year and out of a job several years later. Wall Street's riches to rags stories are just about as numerous as its rags to riches stories.

How heavily regulated is Wall Street?

Wall Street activities are heavily regulated, primarily by the federal government. Similar activities that take place within each of the states are generally regulated by the respective state governments. Regulation applies to new issues of securities as well as to trading securities on the exchanges and among securities dealers.

If there is so much regulation why do people continue to lose money by investing on Wall Street?

Wall Street regulations are designed to ensure that activities are run on the up-and-up and that investors have access to relevant information prior to investing their money. Wall Street regulation is not designed to guarantee that investors do not purchase overpriced stocks and bonds and eventually lose money. There are many hardships that businesses and governments must face and each of these organizations is sometimes unable to pay its bills. There are many reasons why investors can lose money after entrusting their funds to some Wall Street firm. These reasons will be addressed in later chapters.

Why is there so much federal regulation of Wall Street's activities?

Much Wall Street regulation has been spurred by excesses of the organizations that operate on Wall Street. A large part of present-day regulation owes it existence to the major stock market decline and financial panic that commenced in 1929 and extended into the 1930s. The Great Crash along with extensive speculation, fraud, and excesses in the securities markets brought forth a public clamor for additional government regulation.

One of the legislators' first items of business was the creation of the Securities and Exchange Commission (SEC), a powerful organization that to this day serves as the federal government's main regulatory agency for securities trading. Other regulations related to the information that must be provided prior to new securities issues and the methods by which brokers and dealers must operate.

Does Wall Street have any regulations other than those imposed by the federal government?

Most of the institutions that operate on Wall Street have their own regulations that are in addition to federal regulations. For example, a major Wall Street institution such as the New York Stock Exchange has many rules by which employees and other individuals and institutions that are associated with the exchange must abide. Regulations imposed by these institutions often concern ethical standards as well as specific rules on how various activities are to be conducted and supervised.

So is Wall Street a safe place to invest my money?

Wall Street *can* be a safe place for investing one's money, even though many investors have lost a lot of money on Wall Street. A substantial proportion of investment losses occurs because investors become greedy. Brokers sometimes make promises they can't keep and investors sometimes put themselves in very risky situations. Wall Street investing should be combined with some knowledge of the potential consequences and a good dose of common sense.

Chapter 2

WHAT IS STOCK AND HOW IS STOCK VALUED?

CHAPTER SUMMARY

The issuing and trading of stocks are two of Wall Street's major activities. Ownership in stock offers the potential for substantial returns for investors who purchase these securities that represent ownership in businesses. This chapter discusses what stock represents, how stock ownership can produce income for investors, and why stocks can be risky investments.

What is stock?

A share of stock is a unit of ownership in a business. Some businesses have hundreds of shares of stock outstanding while other businesses have hundreds of millions of shares of stock outstanding.

Is there more than one type of stock?

There are two major categories of stock. The majority of stock is of a variety termed *common stock*. If a business has only a single type of stock, this stock will be of the common stock variety. Preferred stock is the second major variety of stock. Both types of stock represent an ownership interest in the issuer.

Preferred stock sounds like it is better to own than common stock. Is this true?

Preferred stock is superior to common stock in some respects, but inferior in other respects. The owners of preferred stock receive their share of the firm's profits prior to the owners of common stock, but the share of profits that preferred stockholders will receive is limited. Thus, even if a business is spectacularly successful, preferred stockholders will continue to receive the same payments. On the other hand, if a business encounters financial difficulties, preferred stockholders are in a better position to have their payments continued than are common stockholders.

Where do shares of stock originate?

Shares of stock are issued by businesses to new owners. Initially, stock is issued when the business is formed and investors must be brought in to supply the business with funds. As the organization grows and requires more capital to purchase buildings, equipment, and items to sell, the owners and managers of the firm may decide to bring in additional funds by soliciting new owners. Thus, many businesses periodically sell additional units of ownership and over several decades a growing firm may issue millions of additional shares of stock.

Why do companies issue stock?

Stock is issued for the purpose of raising money. The money may be needed to build a new factory or the firm's managers may feel that the business should repay some debt. Firms sometimes raise additional funds that are required to buy another business or to expand into foreign countries.

The existing owners of a business will generally bring in new owners only when it is necessary to do so. Most owners of a business do not want to have to share either the profits or control of the business with new owners. Thus, a firm's managers and owners will issue additional shares of stock and bring in new owners only when they believe a higher level of profits and a greater total value for the business will result.

Do investors buy shares of stock directly from the issuing company?

Small businesses will sometimes solicit funds directly from investors. A direct solicitation of funds by selling shares of stock is generally effective only if the business does not need to raise a large amount of money. A large corporation—a firm such as General Electric or Exxon—nearly always utilizes an investment banking firm to assist it in locating investors for a stock sale (see Appendix B). To purchase stock in large corporations, investors must go through a commercial brokerage firm such as Merrill Lynch, Prudential Securities, or Dean Witter.

This means that I cannot simply write to a company and ask to buy shares of the firm's stock?

Most companies are not set up to take occasional orders for shares of stock. Many large corporations do not sell new shares of their stock for decades at a time. These firms find that they are able to finance expansion by methods other than issuing new shares of ownership.

What determines the value of a share of stock?

The value of a share of stock depends upon the value of the business the stock represents and the number of shares of stock that the business has outstanding. The greater the value of a business, the greater the value of the firm's stock. Likewise, the fewer the number of shares of stock that are outstanding, the more valuable each of the shares will be.

Does the value of stock change with the value of the business?

There is a direct relationship between the value of a business and the value of that firm's stock. As a business grows and becomes more profitable, ownership in the business is likely to become more valuable. Conversely, if a business enters a period of falling sales and profits—perhaps because the business encounters a sick economy or more competition—the business is likely to become less valuable and a unit of ownership in the business will have less value.

How is the value of a business measured?

That is a very good question. First, value is a subjective judgment on the part of the person who is making the valuation and even experts will disagree upon the value of any particular business. Although management quality, product quality, customer loyalty, and the amount and quality of assets that are owned all influence the value of a business, the bottom line is cash. The value of a business depends upon the amounts of cash that the business produces and is expected to produce in future years, the time periods when this cash will be available, and the certainty that these cash flows will occur in the amounts and at the times that are forecasted. The problem in valuation is accurately estimating the amounts, times, and certainty of a company's cash flows.

Can you provide an example?

The value of Ford Motor Company depends upon the amount of cash the firm is able to produce and the times when the cash will be available. The greater the amount of cash that Ford can produce and the sooner the cash will be available to the managers for reinvestment or payment to stockholders, the more valuable the firm. Also, the more certain that investors are that Ford's cash flows will occur as forecasted, the more valuable the firm. Because most of the cash produced by Ford is related to automobile and truck sales, the greater these sales are expected to be and the less it costs Ford to produce these sales, and therefore, the greater the amount of cash that the company will be able to generate.

How can I be expected to accurately forecast a giant corporation's cash flows when I can barely balance my own checkbook?

Few people have either the knowledge or the time to accurately estimate a firm's ability to generate cash. Even managers often err in judging the cash flows of their own firm. As a consequence, most investors rely on someone else's judgment or on their own intuition when they select stocks to buy. Additional material on stock valuation is in a later chapter.

Can the value of a particular stock change a lot?

Common stock values are subject to rapid changes. Individual stock issues sometimes double or triple in value in a single year. Unfortunately, shares of stock can also lose one-half or more of their value in a year. Not all stocks exhibit the same price volatility, however. Certain stocks tend to be more stable in price than other stocks.

What does stock look like?

A stock certificate's appearance is similar to a school diploma. It consists of fancy engraving on expensive paper and the owner's name is typed on the face of the certificate. The back of the certificate includes a form for transferring the shares to another investor. This portion of the certificate must be filled out and endorsed when the shares are sold.

If I buy stock, will I receive one certificate for each share that I purchase?

If you purchase stock in a firm you will receive a single certificate that identifies the number of shares you have purchased. For example, if you purchase 125 shares of Delta Airlines you will receive a single certificate for 125 shares. If you purchase 50 shares and then purchase additional shares at a later date, you will end up with two certificates.

If I later decide to sell the stock will I have to sell the entire 125 shares?

You may sell however many shares you wish. If you decide to sell 100 shares you will deliver the certificate to the broker and later receive a new certificate for 25 shares.

Is stock difficult to resell once it is owned?

The ease or difficulty of finding a buyer for your stock depends upon the particular stock that you own. If you own stock in a small firm that has few owners and with few people who know about the company, then you may have great difficulty in selling your shares at a fair price. On the other hand, if you own 200 shares of International Business Machines (IBM) or American Telephone and Telegraph (AT&T), selling the stock is only a call away. That is, you need only call a broker and your stock will likely be sold within a few minutes.

What is a blue chip stock?

A blue chip stock is the stock of a company that has a long history of successful operation and, generally, a long period of uninterrupted dividend payments to stockholders. Blue chip stocks include stocks of companies such as AT&T, Amoco, Exxon, General Electric, IBM, and General Motors (see Appendix C). There are many blue chip stocks in addition to these.

Are blue chip stocks good stocks to own?

Blue chip stocks tend to be conservative investments that vary less in value than the stocks of smaller and newer companies. Blue chip stocks are less likely than most stocks of doubling in value or suffering a big decline in value.

If a company in which I am a stockholder decides to sell additional shares of stock will I be offered the first chance to purchase some of the new shares?

The charters of some firms require that existing stockholders be offered the first opportunity to purchase shares that are part of a new issue. Other firms, although not required to do so, will offer existing stockholders the first chance to purchase new shares that are being offered. Many companies do not follow this policy, however, and offer new shares of stock to outside investors. Even when companies do not first offer new shares of stock to existing owners, these owners generally have the option of purchasing additional shares that are part of the issue or of buying shares from other investors.

How can I profit from owning stocks?

The value of ownership in a business will vary with the profitability of the business. This profitability includes present profits that are being earned, as well as future profits that are expected to be earned. If the profitability of a business improves, the value of the business and the value of the stock will generally increase. Thus, an investor may purchase shares in a company for $25 each and several years later discover that these shares are each worth $40. The difference between the price that was paid and the current value of the shares represents the investor's profit on each share. The more shares that were purchased, the more total profit the investor will have earned. Unfortunately, stock prices do not always move in an upward direction.

Do investors who own stock earn profits from anything other than increases in the value of the stock?

Many companies pay owners a portion of the firm's profits in the form of dividends (see Appendix Y). Companies generally pay dividends by check every three months although some firms make dividend payments twice per year or annually. A few companies actually make monthly dividend payments. A stockholder's total income is the sum of dividend payments plus changes in the stock's value.

Are companies required to pay dividends to their owners?

Businesses are not required to pay out their profits to owners. Many companies retain most or all of their profits to use in purchasing additional assets—buildings, land, and inventories. A rapidly growing company is likely to need all of its profits for reinvestment in more assets. On the other hand, a business with little need for additional assets has less reason to retain profits and is more likely to pay out a large proportion of profits to stockholders.

How can stockholders benefit from not receiving dividends?

If profits are reinvested in additional assets, the firm should grow more rapidly and become more valuable. A greater amount of assets should produce more profits and, eventually, dividends of substantial size. Thus, reinvesting profits ideally will produce even larger dividends down the road. The stockholders surrender something in the present for something of greater size in the future. In the meantime, the owners' stock should become more valuable because the investment community observes the company as one that is growing and earning increased profits.

What if the managers acquire assets that result in losses rather than profits?

If profits were reinvested unwisely, the firm's stockholders would have been better off if the directors had paid the cash to the owners. With dividends, the stockholders would have had the opportunity to reinvest the payments in a more promising asset.

Do dividends change from one year to the next?

Hopefully, the dividends for a particular stock will increase over the years. Increasing dividends are most likely if a firm is able to increase its revenues and profits. Some firms have a proud history of raising their dividends at frequent intervals. Other firms raise their dividend payments sporadically as conditions warrant. A business that has fluctuating revenues and profits (e.g., large profits one year and small profits or even losses the following year) may pay a dividend that is a small part of profits one year and a dividend that is actually greater than the profits that are earned the following year.

Do firms that have been paying dividends for many years ever quit making these payments?

If a firm encounters an unfavorable business environment the directors may decide to conserve cash by omitting dividends. The elimination of dividends is most likely to occur if losses are persistent and directors determine that the outlook is bleak. For example, Eastern Airlines paid dividends for many years before finally eliminating these payments in 1969. Although the airline operated for another 20 years before finally declaring bankruptcy and eventually liquidating, the firm never did paid stockholders another dividend.

Are dividends always paid by check?

Companies sometimes distribute property or additional stock in lieu of cash. Property and stock dividends are most likely when a firm is attempting to conserve its cash. Stock dividends occur more frequently than property dividends, but neither of the options is nearly as popular as cash dividends.

You mean that as a stockholder I may get some equipment or a certificate for additional shares of stock through the mail?

The dividend will not come as a surprise. First, property dividends are very rare, especially for a large company with many stockholders. Stock (as opposed to cash) dividends are more frequent, but firms that pay stock dividends often do so on a regular basis (generally, once a year) so that stockholders are expecting them. In the case of a stock dividend, a stockholder does receive a certificate for additional shares of stock. The number of new shares received will depend upon the number of shares a stockholder already owns.

If a company goes out of business what will happen to the value of its stock?

The reason a company goes out of business is an important determinant of how the owners will fare. If the firm has been suffering losses and borrowing large amounts of money, there is a chance that by the time the business is shut down the ownership value will be zero. The stock will have no value and stockholders will lose whatever amount they paid for the stock. If the owners of a successful company decide to shut down the business, pay its bills, and distribute what's left, stockholders may receive a substantial amount of money. Most corporate liquidations lie somewhere between these two extremes, but since the majority of liquidations occur among firms that are no longer competitive, there is a good chance that the stock of a company that goes out of business will not have much value.

Who decides if a company's stockholders will receive dividends?

A firm's directors determine the amounts and dates for dividends. There is no requirement that a dividend be paid and the directors of a firm may determine that omitting a dividend is in the best interest of shareholders. Many companies have quarterly meetings of directors at which time dividend decisions are made.

I thought stockholders were the owners of a business. Why don't the stockholders vote on whether the firm should pay a dividend?

Stockholders do influence a firm's dividend policy, but in an indirect manner. Stockholders of most businesses have the power to elect a firm's directors. Thus, if a firm's directors anger stockholders by paying too low or too high a dividend (as judged by the stockholders), the stockholders theoretically have the power to elect new directors who are more sympathetic to the stockholders' desires.

What is the relationship between a firm's stockholders, directors, and managers?

Very simply, stockholders elect the directors who set the firm's policies and hire its managers. Although some managers may also serve as directors, being a director is generally a part-time job and most directors are not involved in the day-to-day activities of managing the business. Rather, the directors are charged with overseeing the big picture and laying out broad policy guidelines. The power and effectiveness of directors varies from firm to firm. Some boards of directors are very active while other boards give managers a free hand.

How do stockholders go about electing a firm's directors?

Stockholders generally vote annually on all or a portion of a firm's directors. For example, a company may have sixteen directors, each having four-year terms, with four positions annually up for election. Stockholders of this firm would cast votes for four positions each year.

Rather than being required to travel to an annual meeting to vote for a firm's directors and for other issues that require a stockholder vote, stockholders are sent ballots (termed *proxies*) prior to a firm's annual meeting. These ballots can be marked, signed, and returned to the firm. A proxy gives someone else the power to vote a stockholder's shares.

Who decides upon the individuals who will be candidates for election to a firm's board of directors?

The existing board of directors is likely to appoint a nominating committee that will nominate candidates.

Generally, there is a single nominee for each position so that stockholders are given only the opportunity to either vote for or not vote for each position. Only in rare instances is there an alternate slate of directors. Many investors feel the election of directors is no more than a rubber stamp for the individuals who have been selected by the nominating committee.

How many votes does a stockholder receive?

Most types of stock give stockholders one vote for each director's position up for election per share that is owned. Thus, an investor who owns 200 shares of stock would have 200 votes to be applied to each position. Some firms specify a special voting arrangement in which a stockholder can accumulate the votes to be cast for all of the positions and cast these votes for a single position. Thus, the stockholder noted above could cast 800 votes (200 shares times four positions) for a single position. In general, the more shares a stockholder owns, the more votes and the more power that stockholder has.

Does all stock provide owners with the right to elect directors?

Most, but not all common stocks carry the right to elect directors. Some firms have more than one class of common stock outstanding with one of the classes having all or most of the voting power. Preferred stock may or may not provide owners of the stock with the right to participate in the election of directors. Many issues of preferred stock have no voting rights so that owners of the stock have no influence concerning the selection of directors unless dividends are omitted for a specific number of quarters.

Chapter 3

WHAT ARE BONDS AND HOW ARE BONDS VALUED?

CHAPTER SUMMARY

Bonds represent debt in which the issuers of bonds are borrowers and the bondholders are lenders. A bondholder receives periodic income in the form of interest payments until a scheduled maturity date when the face value of the bond is repaid. Bonds are issued by governments and by businesses, and these securities have become popular investments among investors who desire current income. This chapter discusses the wide variety of bonds that are issued, where these bonds come from, how these securities are valued.

What are bonds?

A bond represents a debt that is owed by the issuer of the bond to the owner of the bond. Most bonds obligate an issuer to make semi-annual interest payments and at a predetermined date (termed the *maturity date*), repay the face value of the bond.

Do bonds represent a particular type of debt?

Various kinds of debt go by different names. *Bond* generally refers to a long-term debt obligation that is secured by some type of asset. For example, an airline may issue bonds to finance the purchase of several airplanes with the airplanes pledged as security for the loan. Long-term loans that are not secured by an asset are termed *debentures*. In the example just noted, the airline might purchase airplanes with the funds that are raised from an issue of debentures, although the airplanes are not pledged specifically as security for the debt.

Certificates that represent loan terms between one and seven years are termed *notes*. Notes are identical to bonds and debentures except that notes are scheduled for an earlier repayment. There are also several securities that represent debt issues with maturities of a year or less. Although there are many variations of debt securities and some of the differences between these securities are important, the basic characteristics of most debt securities are similar and it is convenient to refer to all these securities as bonds.

Where do bonds originate?

Bonds are sold by businesses, the federal government, state governments, cities, counties, hospitals, churches, school districts, and a host of other organizations. Goodyear Tire and Rubber Company, the U.S. Treasury, and the South Georgia Regional Medical Center in Valdosta, Georgia, issue bonds. A bond is no more than a piece of paper that represents a debt on the part of the organization that issued the bond.

How are bonds sold?

Bonds are issued in much the same way that stocks are sold. The organization planning to borrow money will generally employ an investment banker that assists in the fund raising. The investment banker will advise the borrower on the most efficient and least expensive method of locating the needed funds and will take care of the paperwork and other details that precede the sale of the bonds. The investment banker often purchases bonds from the borrower and then resells the bonds to investors (see Appendix D). For example, an investment banker might purchase bonds from the issuer at a price of $990 and resell these bonds to the public for $1,000. Investment bankers sometimes will simply sell the bonds while acting as an agent for the issuer.

Why do organizations issue bonds rather than borrow from a bank?

A borrower may determine that a lower interest rate can be obtained by means of a public sale of bonds. Also, there may be a need to borrow a relatively large amount of money, more than most banks would be willing to lend to a single borrower. Another possibility is that banks may require more security for a loan than a business wishes to tie up. For example, a firm may wish to leave some of its assets unencumbered to support additional borrowing at a later date.

How are bonds different from stock?

Other than the fact that both securities represent financial claims there is very little similarity between stocks and bonds. Stocks represent ownership and have a claim to a portion of a firm's profits. Bonds represent debt and legally obligate the issuer to make certain payments and, eventually, repay the outstanding principal on the loan. Businesses that issue bonds are permitted to use the interest expense as a deduction in calculating taxes. Dividends to stockholders must be paid after taxes have been calculated.

In what denominations are bonds issued?

Corporate bonds are nearly always denominated in multiples of $1,000. Thus, an investor can purchase a single

$1,000 bond or 10 bonds of $1,000 each. In either instance a single certificate that indicates the principal amount of the debt will be issued by the borrower. Bonds issued by state and local governments are nearly always issued in $5,000 increments (e.g., you cannot purchase less than a $5,000 principal amount at a time), while U.S. government bonds are issued in amounts of $1,000, $5,000, and $10,000, depending upon the particular type of bond.

Are bonds always issued at face value?

Although bonds are frequently issued at face value, some bonds are originally sold for less than face value. For example, an investment banker might price a $1,000 principal amount bond at $990. A limited number of bond issues with very low interest payments are issued at large discounts from face value.

Will the borrower be required to repay the face value of the bond even though the bond is issued for less than face value?

The issuer will retire a bond at maturity for face value even if the bond is originally issued for less than face value. Issuing a bond for less than face value means the issuer actually borrows less than the face value of the bonds that are issued. The difference between the amount of money that is taken in when the bonds are issued and the amount that is paid to investors at maturity is an additional cost of borrowing.

Why are some bonds issued at face value while other bonds are issued at less than face value?

The price at which a bond is issued depends upon the bond's interest rate compared to the interest rate that is available on similar securities at the issue date. If a bond's interest rate is competitive with current market interest rates, the bond will be issued at face value. If a bond's interest rate is somewhat less than the market rate at the time of issue, the bonds will be sold at a slight discount to face value.

Do investors receive the bond certificates at the time the money is loaned?

When bonds are initially issued in the primary market there is a lapse of at least several weeks before certificates are printed and delivered to investors. Investors who purchase the bonds (loan the money to the issuer) will have their names imprinted on the certificates.

Can an investor sell a bond prior to the date that the bond matures (the date the loan is due)?

Bond ownership can be transferred at any time so that a bond can be sold prior to the bond's maturity date. Bonds are transferred in a manner identical to that by which stocks are transferred. The owner of the bond endorses the back of the certificate and delivers the security to the brokerage firm that the owner used to sell the bond. The brokerage firm, in turn, will send the certificate to the borrower's transfer agent which will issue a new certificate imprinted with the new owner's name.

An investor who makes a gift of the bond or who sells the bond without the assistance of a broker can send the certificate to the transfer agent.

If I own a $15,000 principal amount of bonds and I have a single certificate will I have to sell the entire amount designated on the certificate?

As with stocks, a bondholder can sell less than the amount represented by a certificate. In this example, you could sell any amount from $1,000 to $15,000. Whether you sell all of your bond or only a portion of the face value of the bond, you will be required to endorse and give up the certificate. For example, if you sell a $5,000 principal amount of the bond you will be required to give up your certificate in order to receive a check for the proceeds from the sale and a new certificate representing a $10,000 principal amount of the bonds.

Do bondholders ever have difficulty locating other investors who are interested in buying a particular bond?

Some bonds are very easy to sell while other bonds may prove to be somewhat difficult to sell. For example, there is a tremendous amount of trading in U.S. Treasury securities so that these bonds are very easy to resell. Some other issues of bonds—bonds of an obscure issuer, bonds that are unrated (a topic to be discussed shortly), bonds that are part of a small issue—may require that the seller accept a reduced price in order to locate a willing buyer.

Can a bondholder require the borrower (the bond's issuer) to redeem a bond prior to maturity?

Only a very few bonds permit the bondholder to force the borrower to repay a loan prior to the scheduled maturity. Bonds with long maturities are generally issued to finance the purchase of long-term assets (e.g., buildings, equipment, land) so that a borrower would find it very inconvenient or even impossible to repay a loan many years before the loan is due. Imagine the bank or savings and loan that holds your home mortgage sending you a letter demanding that you immediately repay the outstanding balance on the loan.

Can a bond's issuer redeem the bond before maturity?

Subject to certain restrictions, borrowers frequently are permitted to repay a loan prior to the scheduled maturity.

Essentially, an early redemption involves a letter to the bondholder requiring that the bond be sent to the issuer. When the borrower receives the certificate, a check for the principal amount of the bond (or for an amount stipulated in the borrowing agreement) will be sent to the investor.

What if I don't want the bond redeemed and fail to send the certificate to the issuer?

After the effective date of a call, the issuer will make no further interest payments. Thus, if you fail to forward your bond to the issuer, you will hold a bond that earns no interest. The principal of the bond will remain unpaid until you surrender the certificate.

Are issuers that redeem a bond prior to maturity required to pay bondholders a premium?

Some early redemptions require the borrower to pay bondholders slightly more than the principal amount of the bonds. For example, the early redemption of a $5,000 bond might cost a borrower $5,300. A penalty is often required when the issuer redeems bonds early in order to take advantage of a lower market rate of interest. Early redemption penalties will be stipulated in the original loan agreement.

How much interest is the issuer required to pay the owner of a bond?

The rate of interest on the loan represented by the bond is determined at the time the money is borrowed and the bond is issued. The dollar amount of interest that will be paid is a function both of the rate of interest (called the bond's *coupon rate*) on the principal of the loan and the principal amount (face value) of the bond. If a $10,000 principal amount bond has a coupon rate of seven percent, the issuer is required to pay of bondholder $700 (seven percent of $10,000) annually. Nearly all bonds stipulate two interest payments per year so the issuer of this bond must pay $350 interest (half the annual interest) every six months.

Does the interest rate on a bond ever change?

Nearly all bonds stipulate an interest payment that remains unchanged for the life of the bond. Thus, an investor who purchases a bond is guaranteed a stream of equal semi-annual payments for as long as the bond is owned.

What if market interest rates increase following my purchase of a bond?

Too bad. You have already committed your funds at what you apparently considered to be a fair rate of interest. You will continue to receive the same semi-annual interest payments until either the bond matures or you sell the bond to another investor. Once a bond is issued, interest payments on the bond do not increase just because market rates of interest increase. Your semi-annual interest payments would also remain the same if market rates of interest fall.

Isn't a fixed rate of interest a good deal for the borrower?

A fixed interest rate makes financial planning easier by allowing a borrower to lock in a constant interest cost. On the negative side, a fixed borrowing rate obligates the borrower to continue making the same interest payments even when market interest rates fall. A business recession might result in lower sales and revenues for a borrower that finds itself no longer able to make the same interest payments.

How does a bondholder fare in the event the issuer goes out of business?

If a business enters into bankruptcy and is liquidated, the bondholders have a legal claim that is prior to the claim of stockholders. However, the claims of bondholders can be quite different depending upon the kinds of bonds that are owned. Owners of bonds that are secured by claims on specific assets generally fare much better than owners of debt securities that are backed only by the issuer's promise of payment.

Is there a possibility that the bonds of a bankrupt business will lose all their value?

It is possible that bondholders could lose their entire investment. On the other hand, it is also possible that bondholders will recover the face amount of the bonds following a bankruptcy of the issuer although there may be some delay in the payments. The circumstances under which firms go out of business will play a large part in how bondholders fare.

What determines the value of a bond?

A bond is desirable for the interest the bond pays and for the principal that will be returned at redemption. When bonds have a similar maturity, larger interest income and greater certainty that the interest payments will occur as scheduled, make the bonds more valuable. For example, a bond with a nine-percent coupon ($90 of annual interest) is more valuable than a bond with a six-percent coupon ($60 of annual interest). Greater income results in a more valuable bond.

The degree of certainty that the bond's issuer will be able to meet the scheduled payments is another important consideration in valuing a bond. The more certain investors are that a bond's payments will occur on schedule, the greater the value of the bond.

Isn't the length of time before a bond is redeemed also an important consideration?

The redemption date is very important in determining the value of a bond. In general, the shorter the time until a bond is to be redeemed the more closely the bond's price will be to the amount that will be received at redemption. If a bond is scheduled to be redeemed next week for $1,000, it will be unlikely the bond will sell for much more or less than $1,000.

Can the market value of a bond change after the bond is issued?

Bond values change with variations in market rates of interest and with changes in the ability of the issuer to service its debt. Either an increase in interest rates or a decrease in the ability of the issuer to make payments will result in a decrease in the market value of a bond. Conversely, if market interest rates fall or if the credit quality of the issuer improves, the market value of the issuer's bonds should increase.

Are the market values of certain types of bonds subject to large variations in market value?

Variations in the market values of bonds varies directly with maturity lengths of the bonds. When there are large increases in interest rates a $1,000 principal amount bond with a 20-year maturity might fall in value by several hundred dollars while a bond with a one-year maturity might fall in value by only $20 to $30. The opposite will occur if market rates of interest decline following the purchase of a bond. That is, when there is a decrease in market rates of interest, a bond that has a long maturity length will increase more in market value compared with a bond that has a short maturity length (see Appendix E).

Does that mean I should not purchase bonds that have long maturities?

Not necessarily. Bonds with long maturities permit you to lock in fixed interest payments for a long period of time. Depending upon your investment needs, you may find this to be desirable. Also, bonds with long maturities often provide a high return compared to bonds with short maturities. In early 1991, Treasury bonds with 20-year maturities provided owners with a yield of approximately eight percent at the same time that Treasury securities with maturities of less than a year carried yields of approximately five percent (see Appendix F). Neither of these yields assumes any gains or losses from changes in market values.

Why are the yields on bonds with long maturities generally higher than the yields on bonds with short maturities?

There are several explanations for the difference in interest rates paid on long-term bonds and short-term bonds. Some experts feel that long-term bonds present investors with more risk—greater variations in market values in addition to the simple fact that more things can go wrong to impair the credit quality of the issuer—so that bonds with long maturities must offer higher yields to attract buyers.

Do bond values vary as much as stock values?

Generally, bonds are subject to much smaller price variations than are stocks. Stocks will sometimes double in value or fall in value by half within a year or less. This amount of price movement for bonds is very unusual and changes in value of 10 to 15 percent are considered large.

A friend told me his broker had located a bond with a very high yield. Is something wrong here?

Any investment that offers an unusually high yield is likely to entail substantial risk. When a bond has an unusually high return, there is likely to be a question concerning the ability of the issuer to make the required payments. Purchasing a bond that pays a 12-percent annual return at a time when most bonds are paying an eight-percent annual return will prove to be a bad investment if the issuer of the high-return bond is soon unable to continue making interest and principal payments.

How can I judge the ability of the issuer to make interest payments and to repay the principal of the bond?

The best way to judge the credit quality of an issuer is to check the credit rating of the bond. There are several firms including Moody's Investor Services and Standard & Poor's Corporation that regularly rate the credit quality of corporate and municipal bonds. The rating classifications of the two firms are slightly different but are comparable. An AAA rating is awarded to bonds of the highest quality. A BBB rating by Standard & Poor's or Baa rating by Moody's is the lowest rating that qualifies a bond as investment grade. Both BBB and Baa are on the fourth from the highest rung on the credit quality ladder. Most investors should probably limit their purchases to bonds rated A or higher (see Appendix G).

Why would anyone want to own a bond rated lower than AAA?

An investor may decide to purchase a bond rated BB or B to earn the higher yield that lower-rated securities pay.

Unfortunately, investors sometimes chase high yields without thoroughly considering the risks that are involved in owning bonds with a low rating.

Is there any risk to owning a bond rated AAA?

Bond ratings are a measure of an issuer's ability to service the interest and principal requirements. Although the rating firms attempt to look into the future when they rate a particular bond, they are not 100 percent successful and some bonds judged as high quality may later prove to be somewhat risky. Also, it is important to understand that the ratings are not designed to measure the volatility of a bond's market value that is caused by changes in interest rates. Even bonds rated AAA are subject to variations in value when market interest rates change.

Why are bonds issued by state and local governments so popular?

The bonds issued by state and local governments (generally termed "municipal" bonds) offer investors one great advantage—the interest on most of these bonds is free from federal taxation and in many instances, is also exempt from state and local taxation. The exemption of interest income from taxation makes municipal bonds very desirable for an investor who has a large tax liability (see Appendix T).

Are state and local government bonds purchased directly from the governmental units that issue the bonds?

State and local government bonds are purchased in the same manner that corporate bonds are purchased. That is, an investor must normally engage a commercial brokerage firm to undertake the transaction although commercial banks also deal in municipal securities. Municipal bonds can be transferred prior to maturity and the bonds pay semi-annual interest just like most corporate and U.S. government bonds.

Are U.S. Treasury securities free of income taxes?

Interest income from U.S. Treasury securities is free of state and local taxation but not free from federal taxation. The exemption from state and local taxation can be a valuable benefit for investors who live in states and cities that have relatively high income taxes. However, state and local income taxes are usually substantially lower than federal taxes so that the state and local tax exemption from owning Treasury securities is not as valuable as the federal tax exemption from owning municipal bonds.

How does the safety of Treasury securities compare to the safety of corporate and municipal bonds?

No security has a higher credit quality than U.S. Treasuries. This high degree of safety applies to short-term Treasury bills, medium-term Treasury notes, and long-term Treasury bonds. It also applies to U.S. Savings bonds, a peculiar investment that cannot be sold or transferred but can be redeemed at the option of the investor.

Even though no credit risk is present, Treasury securities are subject to fluctuations in value caused by changes in market rates of interest. Thus, there is still a risk that an investor who must sell a Treasury bond prior to maturity will receive less than the bond's face value and less than the price that was paid when the bond was purchased. Price fluctuations are quite small for Treasury securities having maturities of two years or less.

Chapter 4

HOW ARE SECURITIES TRADED ON WALL STREET?

CHAPTER SUMMARY

Because of the occasional desire or need to sell securities that are owned, most investors would be hesitant to purchase securities that are not transferable to another investor. One of the important functions of Wall Street is to provide a market for securities that are already in public hands. The best known Wall Street institution, the New York Stock Exchange, is one part of the secondary market that Wall Street provides. This chapter discusses how securities are traded after they have been issued in the primary market.

Are securities easy to sell once they have been purchased?

Most securities can be resold without great difficulty although the ease of locating a buyer can vary depending upon the particular security being sold. In other words, certain securities are easier than other securities to resell. Factors such as the condition of the economy, the availability of credit, and the outlook of investors also plays a part in the ease with which securities can be resold. A security that is easily resold is said to have *liquidity*.

Which securities are relatively easy to resell?

Stocks of large, well-known businesses are generally easy to resell. For example, the common stocks of companies such as Apple Computer, General Motors, AT&T, and General Electric are very actively traded (see Appendix J). Also, many corporate bonds are relatively easy to resell. Treasury bills trade in huge amounts and set the standard for liquidity.

Which securities may be difficult to resell?

Securities that are part of a relatively small issue may be difficult to resell. The common stocks of small companies that have relatively few shares outstanding and even fewer shareholders are not likely to have an active secondary market. Many municipal and corporate bond issues do not have an active resale market.

What happens if I need to sell a security that does not have an active resale market?

A security that does not have an active resale market may have to be sold at a somewhat lower price than you feel is fair. Thus, a stock that appears to be worth $45 per share may have to be sold for $43 or $44, especially if you are in a hurry to sell. Likewise, a bond that should trade for $950 may fetch $920 in a quick sale. If you hold out for a particular price that you feel is fair, it is likely to take longer to sell a security that is not actively traded.

Is it easy to purchase securities that have been issued at some time in the past?

Wall Street deals in thousands of securities that have been issued sometime in the past. Professionals on Wall Street buy these securities and make them available to other investors. In certain respects, Wall Street is a giant clearinghouse for both new and old financial products.

How does the resale market for securities differ from the market in which these securities are originally issued?

Perhaps the easiest way to understand the difference between the secondary market and the primary market for securities is to relate the securities market to the market for baseball cards. If you wish to build a baseball card collection you can purchase packs or boxes of newly issued cards at your local drug store or grocery store, or you can purchase previously issued cards at a card show or card shop. The cards at the card shop are being offered by owners who have accumulated an inventory of baseball cards by buying cards from other collectors. In some instances, the card shop might also stock some cards that other owners have asked the card shop owner to sell for them.

Why would the owner of the shop sell cards for someone else?

The operator of the card shop may agree to take cards on consignment and keep a percentage of the sales price in the event the cards are sold. The owner of the shop does not buy the cards and has no money invested in the cards. Selling cards on consignment reduces the risk to the shop owner because the shop owner doesn't stand to lose money if the cards cannot be sold. Likewise, if a card declines in value the loss is absorbed by the collector who left the card with the shop owner.

How does the card shop relate to the market for securities?

The heart of the secondary market for securities is the many individuals and firms that buy and sell these financial claims. Some firms actually purchase securities from investors and then attempt to resell these securities to other investors. Firms that buy and sell securities act as dealers. In other instances, a firm will purchase a security for another investor in which case the firm acts as a broker. A securities firm that acts as a broker is similar to the card shop that takes investors' cards on consignment. Dealers buy investors' securities for their own inventory and sell from this inventory while brokers bring buyers and sellers of securities together.

Does a securities firm ever act both as a dealer and as a broker?

Many firms perform both jobs. These firms—termed *broker-dealers*—will sometimes buy and sell from their own inventory of securities and will sometimes match buyers and sellers. Nearly all of the large national firms, including Merrill Lynch, Prudential Securities, Shearson, and Dean Witter act as broker-dealers.

Do broker-dealers trade in any and all securities?

Individual broker-dealers specialize in certain securities. For example, a broker-dealer may actively trade 20 stocks that have been selected by the firm. This firm stands ready both to purchase and to sell shares of each of the 20 stocks in which the firm has chosen to make a market.

Does each stock and bond have only a single firm that makes a market in that particular security?

Securities that are widely held and actively traded will have a number of firms that act as dealers. Securities that are relatively inactive may have only a single dealer.

Does it matter to investors how many dealers make a market in a particular security?

The more firms that make a market in a security the more competition there will be in setting a price for the security. Having several dealers as opposed to a single dealer is to the advantage of an investor. Another consideration is that a large number of dealers nearly always indicates that the security is actively traded because an inactive security could not support more than a few dealers.

Can you provide an example of how a dealer might quote the price of a security?

The price a dealer will pay for a security is called the *bid* and the price at which a dealer will sell the security is called the *offer* or the *asked*. The difference between the bid and the offer is termed the dealer's *spread*. A dealer may be quoting an offer of $40 and a bid of $39.50. In other words, the dealer is offering to buy the security at $39.50 per share and to sell the security at $40.00 per share.

How does a dealer determine the price at which to buy and sell a security?

The dealer is constantly attempting to determine a security price that will equate the buying volume and the selling volume. When investors begin selling large amounts of stock to a dealer who does not wish to accumulate additional shares of the stock, the dealer will lower both the bid price and the asked price for the stock. If investors are selling large amounts of a stock to a dealer who is bidding $35 and asking $35.50, the dealer will lower the bid below $35 to attract fewer sellers and lower the offer below $35.50 to attract more buyers. If investors continue to sell more shares than they purchase, the dealer may lower these prices another notch.

Do Wall Street firms make markets in U.S. Treasury securities or is that job reserved for the Treasury or the Federal Reserve?

Treasury securities are initially issued by the Federal Reserve but the secondary market for these securities is provided by Wall Street firms. Dealers in Treasury securities act in an identical manner to dealers in other securities. That is, dealers in Treasuries provide bid and offering prices. The Federal Reserve occasionally buys or sells Treasury securities, but this action is occasioned by a desire to affect the money supply, not act as a market maker for investors.

Are large commercial banks involved in the secondary market for securities?

The big money center banks and large regional banks are active in the secondary market for securities. For example, commercial banks are major players in the municipal bond market. Banks underwrite new issues of municipal bonds and act as municipal bond dealers in the secondary market. Investors can purchase and sell municipal bonds through commercial banks as well as through retail brokerage firms. Commercial banks are also active in trading Treasury securities, and through their trust departments, these institutions trade in corporate bonds and common stocks.

When I sell a security should I expect to receive a price that is at least equal to the price that I paid?

You may receive a price that is more, less, or the same as the price you paid. Securities frequently change in value the same day they are purchased. Thus, you may buy shares of common stock for $60 per share and find that one year later you can sell the shares for $90 each. Or, perhaps, you will only be able to obtain a price of $40 per share. Security prices are in a constant state of movement and there are no price guarantees. An exception is the purchase of a bond for face value when the bond will be held until maturity at which time the face value of the security will be returned.

Are security dealers interconnected?

Securities dealers have instant access to the quotes of competing dealers so that the prices quoted by any particular dealer should not be far out of line with prices quoted by other dealers who make a market in the same security. In fact, dealers often trade with one another when they wish to alter the amount of a security they own. For example, a dealer who wishes to increase his inventory in a particular stock may purchase a large block of the stock from another dealer. Conversely, a dealer who desires to reduce his inventory in a stock near the end of the week may sell a large block of stock to a competing dealer at the other dealer's bid price.

Are most broker-dealers located in the Wall Street area?

Broker-dealers are located all around the country (actually, all around the world) although stocks with primarily a regional interest are likely to attract dealers that are located in the same region of the country as the stockholders. For example, the stock of a large bank headquartered in the Southeast may have dealers in Atlanta, Charlotte, Birmingham, and Nashville, in addition to one or more dealers in New York City.

Do I have to locate one of these dealers in order to sell a security?

Actually, you sell a security in the same way that you purchase the security. That is, you contact a brokerage firm which will, in turn, determine which firms make a secondary market in the security you wish to sell. It may turn out that your brokerage firm also acts as a dealer in the security. If so, the firm may execute the transaction in-house and the confirmation slip sent to you several days following the sale will identify the firm as a market maker in the security.

If my broker does not act as a dealer, will the firm have to contact a firm that does act as a dealer in the stock?

Your brokerage firm will be acting as a broker that brings together you and the dealer. Prior to the transaction the broker will be able to tell you the price the dealer is offering for the security so that you will know how much to expect from the sale.

How do stock exchanges fit into this system?

Stock exchanges are places where many specialized market makers are concentrated in the same location. For example, hundreds of market makers, each making markets in numerous securities, operate on the floor of the New York Stock Exchange. Brokers from all over the world route customer orders to the floor of the exchange where members buy and sell assigned securities.

Is a stock exchange nothing more than a large number of dealers who operate in a single location?

There are differences in the methods by which exchanges operate compared to the methods utilized by dealers in the widely dispersed over-the-counter market. Overall, however, your description is fairly accurate. The following chapter is devoted to the operation of the New York Stock Exchange. Most securities exchanges are operated much like the New York Stock Exchange.

Do the different stock exchanges deal in different securities?

Regional stock exchanges trade securities that have a regional investor following and also trade many securities that have a national following and that are traded on the New York Stock Exchange. For example, the common stock of General Motors Corporation is traded on the New York Stock Exchange and also on regional exchanges.

If a security is traded on a stock exchange is it possible that the security is also traded by one or more dealers outside the exchange?

Many stocks that are traded on one or more exchanges are also traded by dealers who operate outside the exchanges. However, if a particular stock is actively traded on an exchange there is a good chance that the brokerage firm you use will route your order to the exchange rather than to an outside dealer.

Does it matter if I own a stock that is not traded on a stock exchange?

A security that is traded on one of the stock exchanges is said to be a *listed* security. Some experts feel that exchange-listed securities are somewhat more liquid, that is, easier to buy and sell without affecting the price, than are many securities traded only through dealers. On the other hand, many financial analysts make a case that securities traded on the exchanges are so closely monitored by professionals and novices alike, that it is more difficult to locate undervalued securities that are listed. Overall, the average listed stock probably does have more liquidity than the average stock that is traded only by dealers.

Can I be assured of a fair price when I buy or sell a security?

The majority of trades take place at prices that accurately reflect market conditions at the time the trades occur. Unfortunately, there are instances of investors being treated unfairly. Paying an inflated price when a security is purchased or receiving an inadequate price when a security is sold is most likely to occur when a security has a poorly defined market with only a single market maker. If a security has only a single market maker, then the dealer becomes the market and the dealer alone pretty much determines what a security is worth. There have been many instances of dealers bilking investors, especially investors engaged in trading *penny stocks*. Penny stocks are low-priced stocks, often trading at a price of less than a dollar per share. Investors should beware of penny stocks.

I thought Wall Street was heavily regulated. How can investors be swindled if there is effective regulation?

Unfortunately, state and federal regulators cannot at all times keep their eyes on every dealer and oversee trading in every publicly traded stock. History has shown that crooks go where the money is and the money is on Wall Street. The sad truth is many investors get bilked because the investors become greedy and go after investments when they are promised unrealistically high returns.

If the market crashes, can I count on being able to sell my securities?

In the crash of November 1987, it was reported that some security issues could not be sold (or purchased, although few investors seemed to be trying this side of the trade) because dealers were not answering their telephones. This is unusual but it does illustrate that under the worst of conditions the liquidity of many securities may be greatly impaired. On the positive side, virtually anything can be sold if the price is sufficiently low. Thus, even in a crash you should be able to sell securities if you are willing to accept whatever price is being offered by buyers. The problem, of course, is that you may receive a price that is substantially lower than you expected.

Are all of Wall Street's financial deals open to the public or are some transactions restricted?

Investment bankers frequently engage in transactions that exclude the general public. For example, an investment banker may assist a company in raising money by locating an institution or a small number of institutions that are interested either in lending the company money or investing in the ownership of the company. The securities issued to the institutions may never reach the secondary market because the institutions that invest in the company may have no desire to sell the securities.

Does this mean that there will be no dealers in these securities?

If no shares or bonds are available for trading then there will be no need for a dealer to make a market in the securities. Of course, other securities from this same issuer may already be traded by dealers or on a securities exchange.

Are there any other jobs that Wall Street firms perform?

Wall Street firms will sometimes be asked by a company to assist in repurchasing outstanding bonds or shares of stock. The securities may be bought in the secondary market or the firm may make investors an offer to repurchase all or a portion of their securities at a certain price. This latter operation is termed a *tender offer*. Likewise, a hospital or a state may decide to redeem all or a portion of a bond issue.

Why would an organization want to repurchase its own securities?

A company's directors may feel that the price of the firm's shares is inadequate. That is, the directors may feel that investors are not properly valuing the firm's securities. Whether a security is adequately priced is a subjective judgment on the part of the person making the assessment. Most firms that repurchase their own securities do so with the expectation that the security price will increase.

What are takeovers that I have read so much about?

A takeover occurs when one investor or a group of investors takes control of a company from the existing owners and managers. For example, a group of wealthy investors may make a public offer to buy all of the shares of common stock of a company. Should this group obtain a sufficient number of shares of stock to take control of the company, the takeover will be successful and the new owners are likely to install their own directors and managers.

Is Wall Street involved in these takeovers?

An investment group that decides to engage in a takeover nearly always employs the services of one or more Wall Street firms. An investment banking firm will attempt to purchase the stock and will assist in obtaining the financing for investors who are engaging in the takeover. Numerous Wall Street firms earned huge amounts of money in the many takeovers that occurred during the 1980s. Interestingly, the company for which the offer is made (termed the *target firm*) is also likely to hire an investment banking firm, especially if the company's directors intend to fight the takeover.

What if the investors who own a firm do not wish to sell their shares to a group of investors that is attempting a takeover?

Existing owners of a company have every right to decide not to sell their shares. Owners may decide that the price being offered is inadequate. In fact, the managers and directors of a firm often advise owners not to sell their shares because the directors feel the price being offered is inadequate. Directors sometimes advise owners against selling shares in order to obtain a higher bid from the investors who are attempting to purchase the stock. In other takeovers, the directors may simply not want the company to be taken over regardless of the price that is offered.

Are some of these takeovers unsuccessful?

For a variety of reasons, a takeover may fail. Often, the investors attempting the takeover may have difficulty locating the financing that is required to pay for all of the securities. In other instances, the directors of the firm to be taken over may be successful in their attempt to keep stockholders from offering their shares to the investors who are engaging in the takeover.

Are takeovers good for investors?

If the price that is offered for an investor's stock in a takeover is substantially higher than the price at which the stock recently traded, then existing owners of the stock are likely to benefit, at least in the short run. Of course, the group making the offer must feel that the company's shares are undervalued, which means that the investors who sell their shares may not be better off in the long run. Professional opinions vary on whether takeovers are good for the economy.

Chapter 5

WHAT SECURITIES OTHER THAN STOCKS AND BONDS ARE TRADED ON WALL STREET?

CHAPTER SUMMARY

Wall Street is seldom caught short of products to peddle. If investor interest begins to languish in stocks and bonds, you can count on Wall Street to develop new products to hawk. There were an unusually large number of innovative products brought to market in the 1970s and 1980s. One of these—call options—was redesigned and became so popular that some Wall Street professionals claimed these speculative investments diverted capital from stocks and bonds and thereby impeded capital formation by American business. This chapter discusses some Wall Street alternatives to stocks and bonds.

Are stocks and bonds the only securities available from Wall Street?

Wall Street has a product for every need and more than a few products that seem to have no apparent need. There are investments to profit from gold, investments that make money from oil and gas exploration, and investments that attempt to cash in on foreign investing. These investment products sometimes result in investor losses rather than investor profits, but that is part of the game. Many alternative investment products are themselves based on other investment products.

Are all of these different investments actually necessary?

Issuing and trading stocks and bonds is a necessary part of an efficient capitalistic economy. Some of the other investments peddled by Wall Street appear to have little to do with the economy and they mainly serve the public's need for speculation. Of course, the firms that develop investments and the individuals who make a substantial part of their income selling the investments would probably argue that their products are an integral and necessary part of the capitalistic system.

Are these other investments bought primarily by individuals or are they aimed at large institutions such as banks and pension funds?

Some alternatives to stocks and bonds are bought both by institutions and individuals. Other investments are so complicated or involve such a large amount of money that institutions are the main buyers.

What are examples of investments other than stocks and bonds that are offered by Wall Street?

Stock options are one of Wall Street's most popular products. A stock option permits an investor to speculate on the price of a common stock without actually owning the stock. There are also options for other kinds of assets. A stock warrant is another investment asset that provides an investor with an option to purchase shares of stock at a fixed price.

These other products sound more complicated than stocks and bonds. Are they?

Some Wall Street products are so complicated that even the people who sell them often don't have a thorough understanding of their fine points. It is often difficult to value an investment product that is dependent upon the value of some other product. Some complicated investments have values that depend upon the values of other investments which, in turn, depend upon the value of still other assets.

If I don't understand an investment can I trust the judgment of the person who is telling me about the investment?

A good rule is to avoid any investment you don't understand. The less you understand about an investment, the more likely you are to make a faulty decision involving the investment. First, if you don't understand an investment, you will have no idea whether the investment helps to meet your financial needs. Second, complicated investments cause you to be at the mercy of someone who makes a living selling the investment. Also, complicated investments frequently involve commissions that are substantially higher than the commissions to purchase stocks and bonds.

What exactly are options that I have heard so much about?

Options provide an investor with either the ability to purchase a specific asset at a fixed price until a certain date or the ability to sell an asset at a fixed price until a certain date. An option that permits the investor to buy an asset is termed a *call* and an option that permits the investor to sell an asset is termed a *put.* Prior to the early 1970s, options were primarily the domain of professional investors. These same options are now one of Wall Street's most popular products.

What kinds of assets can puts and calls be used to sell and buy?

The most popular and widely available options are puts and calls on common stock. A call option on stock permits an investor to purchase 100 shares of a particular stock at a predetermined price until a certain date. A put option gives an investor the ability to sell 100 shares of a particular stock at a predetermined price until a certain date. Individuals who buy call options are forecasting that the underlying stock will rise in price while individuals who purchase put options are expecting the price of the underlying stock to fall.

Do stock options pay any dividends or interest?

The owners of stock options receive no income payments of any kind. Stock options have value only because they permit an owner to purchase or to sell 100 shares of stock. Even if the underlying stock pays a dividend the investor who owns an option to buy that stock will not receive a dividend.

Can you provide an example of a call?

In early May of 1991, there were calls available to purchase 100 shares of Coca Cola common stock at a fixed price of $55 per share until August of 1991. At the time, the price of Coca Cola common stock was $54.50 per share. Thus, for four months the owner of the call had the right to purchase Coca Cola stock at a fixed price of $55 per share. If the price of the stock increased to $65 within the four months the option owner would be able to buy a stock worth $65 per share for a price of $55.

Where would the stock for $55 come from?

If the owner of the call decides to use the call to purchase Coca Cola stock, the stock will be supplied by another investor who has originated, or *written* the Coca Cola call. The stock does not come from the Coca Cola Company which has nothing to do with the transaction.

Why would an investor agree to sell Coca Cola stock for $55 when the stock was trading for $65?

The investor who acquires the call option pays the writer, or seller, a fee called a *premium* to obtain the call. The seller of the call gives up any potential appreciation above $55 per share in the price of Coca Cola stock in return for a nonreturnable cash payment from the investor who obtains the call.

What happens if the price of Coca Cola stock does not go above $55 during the four months?

In the event the stock price stays below $55 the entire time, the owner of the call will not use the option (why pay $55 for a stock that can be purchased for less?) which will expire without value. The investor who purchased the call will lose the premium paid to the option seller who will keep the premium and not be required to deliver the stock. The option seller may decide to sell a new call option in order to earn some additional premium income.

How does a put option work?

A put option provides the option owner (the person who purchases the option) with the right, but not the obligation, to sell 100 shares of a particular stock at a specified price until a certain date. A put is an option to sell stock while a call is an option to buy stock. Investors purchase put options when they expect the price of a stock to fall and they purchase call options when they expect the price of a stock to increase.

How might an investor use a put option?

Suppose you purchased IBM common stock several years ago for $100 per share and the stock currently trades at price of $125 per share. You think that being an owner of IBM will continue to be profitable but you are concerned about the possibility of a large price decline in IBM stock over the next several months. One possible course of action is to purchase a put option that allows you to sell the stock at a price of $125 per share. During the time you own the option you will be able to obtain $125 per share no matter how much IBM's stock price varies. For example, if the stock falls to $105 per share you have the right to force the investor who sold the option to purchase your IBM stock for $125 per share.

Are there other ways to utilize options?

There are many ways for investors to use options. Puts and calls are sometimes used to speculate on the future price movement of a stock while at other times options are used to reduce the risk of owning another asset. Many of these uses involve complicated investment strategies that are beyond the scope of this book.

Can I buy a put or call and then sell the option before it expires?

There is a great amount of trading in options and most puts and calls are relatively easy to resell prior to expiration.

Should I think about becoming involved in options?

Considering that options are subject to very rapid price movements and that trading in options often involves frequent and relatively large brokerage commissions, most investors would probably do themselves a favor by avoiding these investments. If someone tries to convince you to invest in options, ask yourself why. The answer may be that options are a very profitable product for the broker to sell.

What other kinds of investments are available on Wall Street?

Stock warrants are not as popular as options but warrants can still prove to be interesting investments. Warrants permit an investor to purchase a specific number of shares of stock at a fixed price until a certain date.

This sounds just like a call option. Is there a difference?

First, warrants are issued by corporations that will sell new stock to warrant holders in the event the warrants are exercised. Corporations issue warrants to raise investment capital and, when warrants are issued as an attachment to a bond issue, to lower the interest rate on bonds that are sold. On the other hand, stock options are issued by investors and have nothing to do with corporate fundraising. Second, warrants vary in the number of shares that a warrant holder may purchase. Certain warrants permit an investor to buy three shares of the issuer's stock while warrants from a different issuer may permit an investor to purchase five shares of stock. Warrants are also different from stock options in that warrants generally have a relatively long life and may not expire for several years. Stock options expire in a matter of months.

Why would I want to own warrants rather than the common stock of the issuing firm?

The answer is leverage. A warrant allows someone with a minimal investment to control substantially more stock than if the stock itself is purchased. For example, a warrant to purchase five shares of a stock at $25 per share when the stock trades at $23 allows the owner to control five shares of stock for an investment that may not amount to much more than $15 to $30 (depending upon the life of the warrant). This same amount of money would permit the investor to buy only a single share of stock.

Why would I want to own a warrant that gives me the right to buy stock at a price that is higher than the stock's current selling price?

You are betting (and *betting* is the appropriate term here) that the price of the stock will appreciate to a level above $25 before the warrant expires. Assume that you are able to purchase this warrant for $20 when the stock trades for $23 per share. If the stock subsequently increases in price to $35 per share the warrant will have a value of at least $50 because the warrant permits the holder to purchase five shares of stock at $25, $10 per share less than the stock's market value.

Do warrant owners receive any dividends or interest payments?

A warrant owner is in the same position as the holder of a stock option in that neither investor receives current income of any kind. There are no dividend payments, interest payments, or payments of any kind to the owners of warrants.

Because the warrants are issued by a business, do the warrant owners have any voting rights concerning corporate matters?

Warrant holders have no voting rights. Of course, the warrants may eventually be used to purchase shares of stock which are likely to have voting rights. Warrants make an investor a potential owner, not a current owner of a firm.

Are warrants risky investments to own?

The ownership of warrants entails substantial risk. Warrants are subject to very large price changes so that an investor can purchase a warrant and soon find that the value of the warrant is reduced by half. Many warrants have no value by the time they reach their expiration dates.

If I buy a warrant can I sell the warrant before the expiration date?

Warrants can be transferred to another investor in the same manner as stocks and bonds. Transferability means that you can purchase a warrant from another investor and you can sell a warrant to another investor. The owner of a warrant cannot sell a warrant back to the issuer, however. The warrant is only returned to the issuer when the warrant is used to purchase shares of the issuer's stock.

Options and warrants seem awfully risky to me. Are there any other investments available on Wall Street?

One popular Wall Street investment is bonds that can be exchanged for shares of stock. These bonds—termed *con-*

vertible bonds—offer an investor the safety of a steady stream of semi-annual interest payments and the scheduled return of the principal amount of the bond. The owner of a convertible bond may also swap the bond for a specified number of shares of the issuer's stock. The exchange of the bond for stock occurs at the time chosen by the investor.

This sounds too good to be true. What's the catch?

Convertible bonds allow companies to borrow funds at a lower rate of interest compared to regular bonds. Thus, an investor who purchases convertible bonds will not receive as much interest income as when regular bonds are purchased. The buyer of convertible bonds surrenders some interest income in exchange for the opportunity to trade the bonds for shares of stock. This opportunity to exchange the bond will prove profitable only if the issuer's stock appreciates in value.

If the stock price does not increase and I don't find it profitable to convert the bond, will I eventually receive the face value of the bond?

If a convertible bond is not exchanged for shares of common stock the issuer will be required to redeem the bond at face value at maturity. The payment will be made to the investor who owns the bond at the time of redemption. The maturity date is determined at the time the bond is issued and the date does not change regardless of how many times the bond is resold or who owns that bond at the time the bond comes due.

Can you provide an example of a convertible bond?

Suppose a $1,000 principal amount bond issued by GenCorp has a coupon rate of ten percent and matures in 2010. The bond is convertible into 80 shares of

GenCorp's common stock. This bond will pay the owner $100 annually (ten percent of the bond's $1,000 face value) until the year 2010 when GenCorp will redeem the bond for $1,000. Any time prior to 2010 the bondholder can send the bond to GenCorp in exchange for 80 shares of common stock. If the stock currently trades at a price of $10 per share the bond will have a value of at least $800 because an investor could exchange the bond for $800 worth of common stock. If the stock rises in price the bond should also rise in price.

What about interest payments on the bond?

All the time the stock price is moving up and down the bondholder will continue to receive interest payments. The continuous receipt of interest income is a great advantage of a convertible bond compared to owning shares of the common stock.

If I exchange a convertible bond for shares of common stock and later decide that I made a mistake, can I return the stock and have the bond returned?

The exchange of a convertible bond for stock is not reversible. Once you exchange the bond for shares of stock there will be no more interest payments (you may receive dividends from the stock), there will be no payment of principal at maturity, and you cannot reconvert the stock to a bond. Of course, if the value of the bond rises along with the price of the issuer's common stock there may be no reason to convert the bond until it nears maturity.

Is the price of a convertible bond subject to large, sudden price changes?

Convertible bonds sometimes change suddenly in value but generally not to the extent of the underlying common stock. In the above example, the common stock of GenCorp could be expected to fluctuate to a greater degree than the price of the convertible bond. The greater stability of convertible bond values is one of the reasons that convertible bonds tend to be more conservative investments than the common stock of the same issuer. The security of a convertible bond's interest payments and eventual principal repayment is very important in stabilizing the value of this security.

Are convertible bonds more risky than regular bonds?

Convertible bonds can be risky investments to own for several reasons. First, convertible bonds generally represent unsecured debt. If a company should go bankrupt, owners of the firm's convertible bonds are likely to fare worse than owners of secured bonds in recovering their investments. Also, because convertible bond values are influenced by the values of common stocks—securities that are subject to large swings in value—convertible bonds tend to fluctuate more in price than do regular bonds. On the other hand, convertible bonds give an investor an option on an ownership stake in the issuer. This ownership stake is more likely than bonds to provide some protection against inflation.

Chapter 6

HOW DOES THE NEW YORK STOCK EXCHANGE OPERATE?

CHAPTER SUMMARY

The New York Stock Exchange is the largest organized securities exchange in the United States and one of the largest organized exchanges in the world. Although fewer varieties of securities are traded on the New York Stock Exchange than in the over-the-counter market, trading on the floor of the exchange is the image that many individuals associate most closely with Wall Street. This chapter discusses the organization of the exchange, who works at the exchange, and how securities are traded on the exchange.

Why do I hear so much about the New York Stock Exchange?

The New York Stock Exchange (NYSE) is the oldest, largest, and most active securities exchange in the United States. Daily trading on the exchange regularly exceeds 100 million shares and is sometimes over 200 million shares (see Appendix K). The common stocks of most large publicly owned corporations are traded on the NYSE and both the print and television media often illustrate stories on the economy, the stock market, or some other financial topic with pictures of the floor of the New York Stock Exchange. Although the New York Stock Exchange trades the stocks of only a small percentage of America's businesses, these business are generally the country's largest and best-known firms.

Who owns the New York Stock Exchange?

The New York Stock Exchange is a nonprofit corporation organized in the state of New York. The NYSE has 1366 owners, or members, who are said to own *seats* on the Exchange. The number of members is limited to 1366 so that membership must be purchased from an existing member at a mutually agreeable price. The value of a seat varies with the profitability of membership. When trading is active and profits of existing members are high, memberships are valuable and seats change hands at relatively high prices. When trading activity declines and member profits fall, seats on the exchange sell at low prices. Seats on the NYSE have sold at prices that range from a low of $17,000 to a high of over $1,000,000 (see Appendix L). Owning a seat on the New York Stock Exchange is in many respects similar to owning part of any business.

Can anyone purchase a seat on the New York Stock Exchange?

To qualify for membership, an applicant must be sponsored by at least two current members and obtain the approval of the organization's board of directors. Of course, the applicant must also locate a member who desires to sell a membership. New members are required to pay an initiation fee and all members are assessed annual dues.

Once a seat on the New York Stock Exchange is obtained can the new member simply walk onto the floor and begin trading securities?

The NYSE has different categories of membership and each category entails different responsibilities. The largest number of members act as commission brokers who handle security orders that originate outside the exchange. A commission broker receives orders from a trading desk or from a member of the public by way of a brokerage firm and attempts to obtain the best possible prices on the executions of the orders.

Many members perform as specialists who make markets in securities that have been listed. Each specialist has assigned securities (a typical specialist will trade about 15 stocks) for which the specialist must provide bid and ask prices. Specialists also occasionally act as brokers and match customer orders with orders that have been left by other customers.

The third largest group of members consists of floor brokers who assist other members transact orders. For example, during a time of especially heavy trading, commission brokers may need assistance in executing the orders that flow into the exchange.

Do individuals ever obtain memberships on the New York Stock Exchange to trade only for their personal accounts?

It is rare for an investor to purchase a membership for the sole purpose of trading for a personal account. An exceptional amount of personal trading would be required to justify the high cost of a membership. The majority of investors would incur substantially lower costs by paying a commercial brokerage firm to execute the trades.

Can a member own only a single seat on the exchange?

Some members of the NYSE hold several memberships. Although there are 1,366 memberships, only about 500 organizations hold these memberships. Some of the member organizations are partnerships while other members are organized as corporations.

Do members alone conduct all of the business of the exchange?

Many individuals besides members are required to support the work of the NYSE. For example, a specialist must employ people to assist in the market-making function. Also, personnel are required to deal with the huge amount of record-keeping that is involved in operating an active trading floor. The New York Stock Exchange hires lawyers, accountants, administrators, and so forth.

Is the New York Stock Exchange always open?

The NYSE is open Monday through Friday (except for legal holidays) from 9:30 a.m. to 4:00 p.m. (EST). The exchange is in the process of expanding these trading hours and it is likely that there will eventually be 24-hour trading. The expanded trading schedule is in response to competition from other markets that are open during the hours the NYSE is closed.

How does the New York Stock Exchange decide which securities to trade?

To qualify securities for trading on the New York Stock Exchange, a company must apply for listing and must meet standards that have been set by the exchange.

Standards include minimum requirements relative to earnings, assets, number of shareholders, shares outstanding, and the market value of publicly held shares. Standards set by the exchange tend to exclude the listing of stock by small firms.

Are there any advantages for the company that has its securities listed?

The exchange contends that listing makes securities more marketable (see Appendix J). That is, securities are easier to buy and sell after being listed on the NYSE. The improved liquidity stems from the continuous market that is provided by specialists, the publicity and prestige that results from being listed, and potential investors who might refrain from purchasing securities that are not traded on the exchange. The improved liquidity is good both for investors and for the company that issues the securities because listing is likely to increase the value of the securities which results in lowering the firm's cost of raising capital.

Are the securities of all large companies traded on the NYSE?

Not all large companies have their securities listed on the New York Stock Exchange. Some large firms are owned by only a few wealthy investors so that there is no publicly traded stock. Other firms meet exchange standards but decide not to apply for listing. The directors of these firms apparently feel that investors are just as well served by having the firms' securities traded in the over-the-counter market. Also, the exchange requires that firms with listed securities provide the investment community with a minimum level of financial disclosure. Some firms may not wish to make this disclosure.

Can you provide some examples of large, publicly-owned firms that do not have their securities listed on the NYSE?

Apple Computer (a computer manufacturer), Microsoft Corporation (a computer software company), Roadway (a large trucking company), and MCI Communications (a long-distance carrier) each have stock that is actively traded in the over-the-counter market but is not listed on the New York Stock Exchange.

Are the securities of any foreign companies traded on the NYSE?

Shares of foreign companies are traded on the New York Stock Exchange. Actually, American Depository Receipts (ADRs), or claims on foreign securities that are being held in trust, are traded on the NYSE. ADRs are more easily negotiable than foreign securities at the same time they avoid the problem of becoming involved in dividends denominated in foreign currencies.

Are bonds as well as stocks traded on the New York Stock Exchange?

There are a large number of bonds listed on the New York Stock Exchange although many of these bonds are inactive. Most listed bonds are corporate issues although some foreign government bonds are also traded.

Are listed securities ever dropped from trading?

If a company goes out of business or is purchased by another firm, the stock will no longer be available for trading. Some stocks that no longer meet exchange standards are de-listed. For example, a company may repurchase a relatively large number of its own shares such that the remaining shares of the stock that are outstanding become relatively inactive. Another possible reason for de-listing is a failure of the issuer to promptly disclose required financial information.

If a security I own is de-listed how will I sell it?

A security that is de-listed by the New York Stock Exchange is likely to be listed on some other exchange and to be traded in the over-the-counter market.

How are securities traded on the exchange?

The New York Stock Exchange is operated as an auction market. Stock is sold to the highest bidder and bought at the lowest offering. The heart of the exchange is the specialist system in which specialists act as market makers and as brokers for orders that flow into the exchange. Specialists function as dealers when they purchase stock for their own account or sell stock from their own account. For example, a specialist may receive an order to purchase 200 shares of stock that cannot be matched with an offsetting order to sell 200 shares of the same stock. Without the offsetting order, the specialist will fill the order by selling the 200 shares from the specialist's account.

Where do the specialists' orders come from?

Specialists' orders originate at retail brokerage firms around the world. An investor's order to purchase stock is sent to the brokerage firm's trading desk where it is routed to a dealer or to an exchange where there is a market in the security. If the order is routed to the New York Stock Exchange (as opposed to being routed to another exchange or to a dealer in the over-the-counter market), the firm's commission broker will take the order to the specialist who makes a market in the stock.

With hundreds of millions of shares traded each day, don't all these commission brokers get in each other's way as they carry orders to the specialists?

Many orders of modest size are conveyed to the specialist through the exchange's Designated Order Turnaround (DOT) automated execution system. The DOT system routes orders directly from a member firm to the appropriate specialist. Thus, a DOT order reduces confusion on the exchange floor by eliminating the need for a commission broker to walk to the specialist's post.

What do you mean by specialist's *post*?

The specialist's *post* refers to the desk where the specialist conducts business on the floor of the exchange. The specialist who makes a market in a particular stock is at the same location on the floor of the exchange each day. Thus, commission brokers know where to go to execute an order for any given stock.

Does the commission broker represent the investor who enters the order?

The commission broker does indeed represent the investor whose order is taken to the specialist. If the investor has entered an order to purchase a security, it becomes the job of the commission broker to obtain the lowest possible price. If the investor has placed an order to sell a security, it is the commission broker's job to obtain the highest possible price.

Do the specialist and commission broker meet and negotiate a trade at the specialist's post?

If specialists and commission brokers negotiated every order the system would soon come to a standstill. The specialist quotes a bid and ask price such as "$25 bid and

25 1/8 ask." In this case the specialist offers to buy stock at $25 per share and sell stock at $25 1/8 per share. This quote leaves no room for negotiation because there is no price between the bid and ask. If the difference between the two prices is larger than an eighth, the commission broker might ask the specialist to raise the bid by an eighth (on a customer order to sell) or to lower the ask by an eighth (on a customer order to buy).

Can a specialist refuse to buy or sell a stock in which the specialist is a market maker?

Specialists are required to furnish bid and ask quotations and to provide a continuous market in the stocks that are assigned. Specialists must fill orders (at the quote) either by matching orders from their book or by buying or selling for their own account.

As an investor do I have any control over the price at which I buy or sell a security?

Although it is unlikely that you can influence the price at the time the order is entered, you can specify an acceptable price. For example, on an order to sell 100 shares of AT&T stock, you can specify on the order that the stock not be sold at a price of less than $35 per share. Likewise, if you are interested in buying stock you can specify that the stock not be bought for more than $34 per share. An order with a minimum selling price or a maximum purchase price is called a *limit order*.

What if the specialist will not pay $35 per share for my stock?

If your asking price is higher than the specialist's bid (the price at which the specialist will buy), the order will be entered in the specialist's book. Every specialist maintains a book for orders that have specified a price that does not allow for immediate execution.

How long will the specialist keep the order?

You may enter a *day order* in which case the order remains effective only for the day it is entered. If a day order is not executed during the day the order can be re-entered the following morning. An alternative to a day order is a *good-till-canceled order* that will remain active until the order is executed or until you request that the order be canceled.

Can you provide an example of how a limit order might work?

Suppose you enter an order to buy 100 shares of IBM common stock at a maximum price of $105 per share. At the time your order arrives on the floor of the exchange the specialist is quoting IBM at $107 1/2 bid and $107 3/4 ask. Your order cannot be executed because the specialist is offering to pay a higher price than you specify in the order. Your order will be placed in the specialist's book and will eventually be executed if the price drops to $105. Of course, if IBM stock does not fall to $105 and, instead, begins rising, you will be on the sidelines watching as your order stagnates in the specialist's book.

Am I sure to get the stock if the market price drops to $105?

Not necessarily. Orders are filled in chronological order and there may be limit orders ahead of yours to buy at $105. For example, there may be many orders in the specialist's book to buy IBM at $105 at a time when only 300 or 400 shares trade at that price.

What happens if I don't specify a price?

An order on which no price is specified is termed a *market order*. A market order is executed at the best possible price at the time the order arrives on the floor of the exchange. In practice, the best possible price means that you will pay the price that is offered by the specialist. When a stock is actively traded a market order will probably result in buying or selling a stock at the same price as the last trade. However, the danger of using a market order is that you may end up paying a little more than you expect when you buy stock and you may receive a little less than you expect when you sell stock.

Is it better for me to enter a market order or a limit order?

If you are buying or selling a fairly active stock and are an investor who tends to hold securities for relatively long periods (say, several years) you should probably enter market orders. Attempting to save a fraction of a dollar per share when you plan to hold a security or have held a security for several years is shortsighted. If you are entering an order for an inactive security or you are planning a short holding period you should consider entering a limit order.

Should I limit my holdings to stocks that are listed on the New York Stock Exchange?

Not necessarily, although NYSE listed stocks are not a bad place to start investing. As you build a portfolio of stocks, you are likely to want to consider adding stocks that trade on one of the other exchanges or in the over-the-counter market. Limiting securities to those listed on the New York Stock Exchange excludes too many investments that have the potential to help meet an individual's investment goals.

Chapter 7

How Do I Locate a Broker and What Can a Broker Do for Me?

Chapter Summary

A broker is the investor's connection with Wall Street. Brokers provide advice, transmit orders, locate information, and take care of the snafus that will almost surely pop up from time to time. The quality of brokers and the firms that employ them varies widely. Some brokers provide reduced services at a substantial savings in commission rates. Other brokers are employed by firms that offer virtually every investment product and service imaginable. This chapter discusses the services that brokers provide and the fees that are charged.

Do I have to go through a brokerage firm to buy or sell securities?

Except in rare instances an investor must employ the services of a retail brokerage firm to buy or sell securities. Brokerage firms have access to the over-the-counter market and to the trading floors of the stock exchanges.

How do I locate a brokerage firm?

Brokerage firms are listed in your local telephone directory yellow pages under *stocks and bond brokers*. If you reside in a small town that has no local brokerage firm you are likely to find several advertisements from brokerage companies in nearby towns. Many firms have toll-free telephone numbers or will accept collect calls. You will find numerous brokerage firm advertisements in most metropolitan newspapers and in financial publications such as *The Wall Street Journal*. Of course, you can always ask friends for recommendations.

Does it really matter what firm I use?

The choice of a brokerage firm can be important. Firms charge different commissions for identical transactions. Buying 100 shares of a $40 stock may involve a commission of up to $100 or more at some firms while other firms may charge a fee of $35 to $40. Commission differences are even larger for transactions that involve a greater amount of money. The more trades you intend to make the more that commission rates should become a factor in selecting a brokerage firm.

Brokerage firms differ in the quantity and quality of services they provide. Many firms that offer the very lowest fees may also provide a reduced level of personal service compared to firms that charge higher fees. Even firms that charge relatively high commissions may differ in the services and products they provide.

How do I locate a discount broker?

If you live in a large city, there should be discount brokers listed in the telephone yellow pages. If you live in a more rural area, you can find advertisements placed by discount brokers in investment publications such as *The Wall Street Journal* or *Barron's*. Call several of the listed numbers and ask for a kit for opening an account. The kit should detail the services that the firm provides and the commissions that it charges (see Appendix M).

What investors are best served by using a discount broker?

Discount brokers are appropriate for investors who on their own decide which securities to buy and sell. Discounters are set up to transact orders but most discount brokerage firms do not maintain a research department and do not offer advice on which securities to buy and sell. Reduced expenses allow these firms to offer relatively low commission rates and still earn a profit.

Are discount brokers an appropriate choice for novice investors like myself?

Investors who have limited knowledge of the market and of the kinds of securities that are available are probably best served by utilizing a full-service brokerage firm. Although the fees at full-service firms are higher than the fees charged by discount brokers, the counseling that many full-service firms offer is sometimes worth the extra expense.

If I go to a full-service firm how will I come into contact with a broker?

When you walk into a brokerage firm, the first person you encounter will be the receptionist. At that time, you inform the receptionist you would like to talk with a broker. You may want to add that you prefer that the broker be female (male), young (mature), someone who is particularly versed in bonds (stocks), and so forth. It is both to your advantage and the firm's advantage that you are matched with a compatible broker.

What should I say to the broker?

A broker will want to know what kind of investor you are. This will include some idea of your income, your assets, and your investment goals. A broker cannot provide adequate investment advice without the bare essentials of your financial status. You will also be asked to complete and sign some papers to open an account.

Will I be able to buy or sell a security the same day that I open the account?

You will be able to enter an order after opening an account. Some firms require that new customers make a deposit of cash or securities into their account prior to the first trade. The firms are concerned that new customers may enter an order but fail to settle up when the money is due. Such occurrences are most likely when a customer enters an order to buy stock only to see the stock price decline immediately after the purchase date.

What are the rules on payment?

Investors are required to pay for stocks and bonds within five business days of the transaction. For example, if you purchase 100 shares of a stock on Monday, in most instances you will be required to have the payment in the hands of the brokerage firm by the following Monday. A legal holiday will delay the payment by a day and weekends are not counted.

If I am interested in investing but don't know what to purchase will the broker have some ideas to get me started?

One thing you don't have to worry about is the possibility of a broker running out of ideas on how to invest your money. If you have a moderate income and a nominal amount of funds available for investment and don't already own any other securities, there will be a good chance the broker will recommend that you consider shares in a mutual fund. Mutual funds are discussed in a later chapter.

Any hints on how I should react to the broker's recommendations?

You can learn a lot about your broker at this first meeting so keep your eyes, ears, and mind open. You will probably be best served by taking home the broker's recommendations in order to give yourself time to digest the encounter. There is certainly no obligation on your part to enter an order at the time the account is opened.

Are all brokerage accounts the same?

One decision you will have to make is whether to open a cash account or a margin account. A cash account requires that you pay in full for any securities you purchase while a margin account permits you to pay only a portion of the purchase price. To open a margin account you will need to sign a margin agreement that spells out the details of the account including how interest is charged on money that is borrowed.

How does a margin account work?

Suppose you have $5,000 available for investment and are interested in purchasing the common stock of Ford Motor Company which is trading at a price of $40 per share. With a cash account you will be able to purchase 125 shares ($5,000/$40) of stock. A margin account that permits you to borrow up to 50 percent of the amount invested (the percentage is set by the Federal Reserve) allows you to purchase twice as much stock, or 250 shares. Thus, with a margin account you can purchase up to $10,000 worth of Ford stock, half with borrowed money and half with your own funds (see Appendix N).

Is it a good idea to buy securities with borrowed money?

Purchasing securities with borrowed money is very risky. Buying twice as much of a security by borrowing 50 percent of the cost doubles the gains and losses compared to paying in full (and purchasing half as much stock). In the above example, suppose the price of Ford stock drops from $40 to $35 per share soon after you buy it. If you paid in full for 125 shares you would have a paper loss of $625. Utilizing borrowed funds to purchase 250 shares would produce a paper loss of $1,250. If the stock had increased in price following your purchase you would have twice the paper profits (compared to paying cash) if you purchased the stock on margin. The bottom line is that most investors should probably stay away from purchasing securities on margin.

Can I borrow against my securities and use the borrowed funds for some other purpose than to buy more securities?

Securities are excellent collateral for a loan. If you maintain a margin account and have securities in the account, you can borrow against the securities and use the proceeds of the loan for any purpose you desire. This assumes that you are not already using the securities as collateral for another loan. Suppose you own 500 shares of a stock that is listed on the New York Stock Exchange. If the security is in your brokerage account, it may be used as collateral for a loan. You simply ask your broker to send you a check. If you have taken delivery of the shares which are currently in a lock box, you will need to deposit the shares into your brokerage account before borrowing funds through your broker. An alternative is to deliver the certificate to your bank and obtain the loan from that source.

Why would I want to borrow against my securities and use the borrowed funds for some purpose other than investing?

It may be less expensive to borrow from your brokerage account. This is especially likely if the funds are used in place of credit card borrowing. In fact, if you have an outstanding balance on one or more credit cards, you can almost surely save money by borrowing against your securities and using the proceeds of the loan to pay off credit card balances. Of course, you will need to determine the rate you will be charged on a margin loan or a bank loan using the securities as collateral in order to compare the cost with some other source of borrowed funds.

Will most brokerage firms be able to transact an order on any exchange?

Brokerage firms, either full-service firms or discount firms, will be able to enter orders on any national or regional exchange or in the over-the-counter market. From the standpoint of carrying out orders for most securities including stock, bonds, options, and warrants, nearly all brokerage firms offer virtually identical service.

Are the certificates for securities that I purchase kept by the brokerage firm or sent to me?

At the time you open an account you will be asked if you want securities delivered (e.g., sent to you by mail) or kept in your account. If you open a margin account and borrow a portion of the cost of securities that are purchased, you will be required to leave the securities in the account as collateral for the loan. If you open a cash account or if you have no need for collateral in a margin account you can choose to have certificates delivered.

Should I leave my securities in the account or should I have them delivered?

It will save trouble on your part to leave securities in the account. Leaving securities with the broker allows the firm to take care of safekeeping the securities and to collect dividends and interest payments. Taking delivery of securities means that you will need to ensure that the certificates are kept in a safe place. Another consideration is that taking delivery of a security requires that you deliver the certificate to the broker at the time you sell the security. This means making a trip to the brokerage firm or incurring the cost of sending a registered letter.

What happens if I take delivery and then lose a certificate?

Replacing a certificate requires that you post a bond costing about two percent of the security's market value. Thus, if you lose a certificate for 200 shares of a stock that sells for $30 per share, you will be required to purchase a $6,000 bond at a cost of about $120. This is a one-time cost on your part.

Will the brokerage firm charge a fee to keep my securities?

Various brokerage firms have different policies regarding account maintenance fees. Many firms levy an annual fee of from $35 to $60 for accounts that have no activity for a one-year period. An investor who undertakes at least one trade per year will avoid this fee. The possibility of an account maintenance fee is an important topic to discuss with a broker before opening an account.

If I leave securities in my account what will happen to dividend and interest payments? Also, how can I vote my shares?

When securities are left in an account, dividends and interest will be paid into the account. You can leave standing instructions that cash balances in the account be forwarded to you. Most firms will send checks near the first day of the month following receipt of dividends and interest. With respect to voting your shares, all reports and proxies will be forwarded to you by the brokerage firm. Thus, you should receive all of the financial reports (sometimes late) that are normally sent directly to stockholders and you will retain your right to vote your shares of common stock.

Can dividends and interest that are in my account be reinvested in a money market fund?

Virtually all brokerage firms provide customers with access to money market funds. Some firms automatically sweep a customer's cash balances into a money market fund. A number of these firms even permit investors to choose among a tax-free fund, a government securities fund, and a regular money market fund. At the time the account is established the customer can direct that all dividends, interest payments, and proceeds from sales of securities be swept into the fund. Some brokerage firms require that customers direct their broker to transfer cash balances to a money market fund each time cash is credited to the account. This procedure can be a pain for both the investor and the broker.

A friend told me about a special brokerage account that includes a credit card and a checking account. What kind of account is this?

Some of the larger brokerage firms offer an account in which all cash balances are automatically swept into a money market fund (see Appendix O). Balances in the money market fund, in turn, can be accessed by checks or by a credit card (some firms use a debit card), both of which are part of the account. This all-in-one account goes under a variety of names although the accounts are pretty much all the same.

Is there an extra charge for one of these accounts?

The annual charge generally ranges between $50 to $100 depending upon the firm. Some firms offer the account with a debit card at a reduced fee. Opening one of these accounts requires an initial deposit of securities or cash that ranges from $5,000 to $20,000 (depending upon the firm).

Is my brokerage account insured in the same manner as my bank account?

There is insurance coverage for investor losses that result from brokerage firm collapses; however, the coverage does not extend to losses caused by declines in security values. In 1970, Congress established the Securities Investor Protection Corporation (SIPC) as part of the Securities Investor Protection Act. The insurance fund covers investor losses of up to $500,000, including a maximum of $100,000 in cash. This insurance is similar to FDIC insurance at commercial banks.

How can I lose money if my brokerage firm collapses? Won't the securities that I own continue to have value?

In the event that the brokerage firm fails and regulatory authorities are unable to locate a customer's securities or cash, the SIPC is designed to take care of the losses up to the maximum amounts specified. This insurance is especially valuable for investors who leave securities in a brokerage account. Some brokerage firms also carry additional insurance through private carriers that provide protection above the SIPC amounts.

Brokerage firms don't provide insurance to cover losses in the market value of my securities?

Unfortunately, there is no insurance to cover losses that are caused by bad investment decisions. The SIPC was created to maintain investor confidence in the financial markets, not to guarantee that investing is a one-way road to profits.

Chapter 8

HOW DO I INTERPRET THE FINANCIAL PAGES?

CHAPTER SUMMARY

To many novice investors, the daily financial pages appear to be printed in a foreign language. A little study can go a long way in unraveling the complexities of both security price listings and measures of market activity. This chapter discusses how to locate and interpret some of the most frequently sought after financial data that regularly appear in the business section of most large newspapers.

Where can I locate price quotations for stocks in which I have an interest?

If it is a widely-held security you can start by looking at price quotations on the New York Stock Exchange. Similar quotations are also provided for stocks listed on the American Stock Exchange and stocks traded in the over-the-counter market. All of these listings are carried by *The Wall Street Journal* and in the financial sections of most metropolitan newspapers. If you can't locate the *Journal* at a newsstand, try your local library. More comprehensive listings are published on a weekly basis (each Monday) in *Barron's*.

How will I know whether a stock is traded on the New York Stock Exchange, the American Stock Exchange, or in the over-the-counter market?

The easiest way to find out where a stock is traded is to look in each of the three listings. If it is a large, widely-held stock, the chances are it is traded on the NYSE. In fact, the NYSE is probably a good place to start when you are searching for the price of a stock. If you don't locate the stock on the New York Stock Exchange, next try the over-the-counter listings.

What if the stock isn't listed in any of the three markets?

If you can't locate a stock in any of these listings, then the stock is probably traded in the over-the-counter market. Most financial pages contain an abbreviated OTC listing for stocks, and there is a chance your stock isn't included in the listing. Another possibility is that your stock did not trade on a particular day. If you can't locate the stock after several days, you can call a brokerage firm and ask where to look for the price. One last thing to keep in mind is that most listings abbreviate a firm's name so that you may be overlooking a particular stock by mistaking an abbreviation for a different company. Listings are arranged in alphabetical order as if the firm's name is spelled out in full.

Is a security price always in the same place each day? For example, if my stock is listed on the American Stock Exchange today, will it be listed on the same exchange tomorrow or next week?

Once in a great while a firm will apply to have its stock listing moved to a different exchange. For example, a firm might change its listing from the American Stock Exchange to the New York Stock Exchange. However, changing a listing is generally a once-in-a-lifetime event for a company. Thus, you should look for your stock's listing in the same location each day.

Once I obtain a newspaper and locate the stock, how do I interpret all of the information?

Different publications include different pieces of information with some publications offering much more complete information than other publications. At the very least, the listing will include the stock's closing price from the previous day's trading. The closing price represents the last price at which the stock traded on the previous afternoon.

Stock prices are quoted in eighths of a dollar so that a quotation of 25 3/8 is equal to $25.375 per share. Thus, if you own 100 shares of a stock that has a closing price quotation of 34 5/8, the securities have a total value of $3,462.50. At least, the security had this value at the close of trading the previous afternoon.

What about the fraction labeled *net change* that follows the closing price?

Net change represents the price change between the closing price shown in the quotation and the closing price the previous day the security traded, generally the most recent trading day. Suppose Thursday's paper shows the closing price for Goodyear stock was 19 1/2 with a net change of + 3/4. The quotation indicates that Goodyear's last trade on Wednesday occurred at $19.50, a price that was $ 0.75 per share higher than Tuesday's closing price. An owner of 100 shares of Goodyear stock was worth $75 more on Wednesday evening compared to Tuesday evening. If the net change column is blank or shows a series of dots, the stock closed at the same price as the previous day's closing price. In other words, the net change is zero.

My morning paper also lists each stock's volume. What does this mean?

Volume is the amount of trading that takes place on a particular day. The volume shown is in units of 100 shares. Thus, if a stock's volume column indicates *120* there were 120 times 100, or 12,000 shares of the stock traded on that day. Although a trade of 100 shares involves both a buyer and a seller, the trade is treated as only 100 shares in trading activity.

Why is volume listed in 100 share units?

Stocks normally trade in units of 100 shares. Also, if the column listed trading in full, many of the volume numbers would be quite large because on a busy day some stocks trade over a million shares.

What other information is provided?

Newspapers that devote substantial space to stock listings often include the high and low prices for the day and, less frequently, the high and low prices for the last 52 weeks. The daily price range may be of interest to an investor who has entered an order to buy or sell the stock that day. The price range for the previous 52 weeks can indicate if a security is in an uptrend or downtrend.

What do you mean?

Some investors are interested in comparing the current price of a stock with the stock's price range during the last twelve months. For example, if a stock sells at near its yearly high, the stock is likely to have an upward price momentum (e.g., be in a uptrend) that makes it an attractive security to own. Being able to compare a stock's current price with the price range during the past year adds to the value of price data.

What is the P/E ratio?

Some stock listings include a column that displays each stock's P/E ratio. The P/E ratio—an abbreviation for the price-earnings ratio—is calculated by dividing the stock's closing price by the firm's earnings per share. In other words, the P/E ratio indicates the price at which the stock sells compared to each dollar of net income (per share) the firm earned. An Investor who pays a high price for a dollar of earnings (e.g., the P/E ratio is relatively high) anticipates that the firm's earnings will be growing. A low P/E ratio generally indicates pessimism over a firm's prospects, although some investors are attracted to stocks with low P/E ratios.

Do the listings provide information on a firm's earnings per share?

Earnings per share (EPS), the amount of net income after taxes divided by the outstanding shares of common stock, is not listed separately, but this statistic can be calculated if the P/E ratio is listed. Earnings per share equals the closing stock price divided by the P/E ratio. For example, if the NYSE listing for Southern Company (an Atlanta-based electric utility) indicates a P/E ratio of 10 and a closing price of $25, the firm's earnings per share is $25/10, or $2.50.

Does the dividend information relate to last year's dividend?

Unless there is something to indicate otherwise (generally a letter beside the dividend amount), the dividend entry designates a stock's current annual dividend. For example, an entry of $1.80 indicates that an owner of the stock is currently receiving an annual dividend of $1.80 for each share owned. It is important to remember that dividends are paid quarterly so that one-fourth of the $1.80 is paid every three months.

Some papers also include a column to indicate a stock's yield. The yield refers to the return a current stockholder is earning from the indicated dividend and is calculated by dividing the annual dividend by the closing price. For example, if a stock with a closing price of $25 has an indicated dividend of $1.50, the yield is $1.50/$25, or six percent.

Does the financial page indicate the date when the next dividend is paid?

To determine dividend dates you will need to refer to *Barron's* or to more specialized publications such as the *Value Line Investment Survey* or *Moody's Stock Handbook*. Each of these publications can be found in nearly any public library or college library.

Why is there nearly always a listing of the most-active stocks?

Many investors are interested in knowing which stocks are heavily traded on a particular day (see Appendix J). Some investors feel that trading volume is an important consideration in singling out stocks to buy or to sell because substantial trading volume often indicates that something important has occurred. For example, a company may have announced a dividend reduction or made an earnings announcement that has surprised financial analysts. Perhaps an offer has been made by another firm to buy out a company's shareholders at an inflated price.

Most financial pages seem to publish several market indexes. Why is this and what do these indexes indicate?

Stock market indexes are intended to indicate how stock prices stand relative the level of stock prices at some other time (see Appendix I). For example, a newscaster may announce that an index is up 40 points to 2440. That means the index has increased from 2400 to 2440, or 1.7 percent during the trading session. An index is calculated by combining the prices of selected stocks that, taken as a group, provide an indication of movements for the entire market.

Are the stocks included in an index ever changed?

There are infrequent changes in the securities that make up an index or average. For example, a stock may no longer be traded because the company has gone out of business or been merged into another company. Also, a firm's directors may sell some of the company's assets so that the company no longer satisfies the requirements for a stock to be included in a particular index.

What are some of the popular indexes?

The Dow Jones Industrial Average, frequently referred to as the *Dow*, is the measure of stock prices used most frequently by the media. Newspaper headlines that exclaim *Market Down 90!* and *Dow Skyrockets to New High* are both referring to the Dow Jones Industrial Average (sometimes shortened to DJIA). The DJIA is calculated using the prices of 30 high-quality stocks listed on the New York Stock Exchange (see Appendix P). No adjustments are made for the size of each firm or for a firm's number of shares outstanding. Because of the limited number of stocks and the similar nature of the stocks that are used in calculating the average, some experts consider the Dow to be a better measure of what is happening to blue chip stocks than a measure of what is happening to the overall market. Dow Jones & Company also calculates separate averages for utility stocks, transportation stocks, and the market as a whole.

Is there a more accurate measure of market movements than the Dow?

Many financial analysts prefer the S&P 500 index that is calculated by Standard & Poor's Corporation. Although the S&P 500 is also heavily weighted with blue chip issues, the greater number of issues (500 as opposed to 30) and the greater diversity of issues that are included in the S&P, allow this index to provide a better picture of what the overall market is doing. The S&P 500 takes into account the outstanding shares of each stock as well as the price of the respective stock. Like the DJIA, the S&P 500 is published by most daily newspapers.

Are there any other market measures I should examine?

Many financial analysts consider a comparison of the number of stock issues that advance in price and the number of issues that decline in price during a trading session to be an important measure of market strength. If the number of advances substantially exceeds the number of declines, the market can be exhibiting an upward momentum that may not be clearly evident examining by the price averages.

Where do I locate the number of advances and declines?

Advances and declines are generally contained in a small section of most financial sections termed *Market Diary* or *Market Activity*. This same section will also often contain the number of issues traded, the number of issues making new highs, and the number of issues making new lows. Each statistic provides an indication of the market's direction. Information on advances and declines is also generally provided for securities traded on the American Stock Exchange and in the over-the-counter market.

How do I read the bond quotations?

Bond prices are quoted in percent of par value and, like stocks, are in eighths (see Appendix Q). Thus, a closing price of 95 3/8 indicates the bond's previous day's close was at 95.375 percent of $1,000 (corporate bonds are denominated in units of $1,000), or $953.75. A closing price of 103 1/4 indicates that a bond's last trade occurred at a price of $1,032.50. An entry of + 1/4 in the net change column indicates the bond closed up by a quarter of one percent of $1,000, or $2.50 compared the closing price the prior day. A net change entry of - 2 1/4 indicates a daily decline in price of $22.50 per $1,000.

What is the meaning of the numbers located directly to the right of a bond's issuer?

Because many companies have more than a single bond issue, it is sometimes necessary to include information that differentiates among issues. Bonds are differentiated by coupon size and maturity date. Thus, an IBM bond appearing as *IBM 9s98* indicates the bond issue has a nine-percent coupon rate (i.e., pays annual interest equal to nine percent of the bond's par value, or $90) and matures in 1998. Obtaining the exact maturity date requires checking a more detailed publication such as *Moody's Bond Record*.

Is the entry for current yield calculated by dividing annual interest by the bond's closing price?

Exactly. For example, a bond with an eight-percent coupon and a closing price of 94 has a current yield of $80/$940, or 8.5 percent. When *cv* is listed in place of a percentage it indicates that the bond issue is convertible into shares of common stock.

Do I have to multiply the volume by 100 as is done with stock volume?

Bond volume is listed in full. That is, if the volume column indicates 35, then 35 bonds were traded the previous day. Many financial listings do not indicate bond volume or the daily and annual high and low prices.

Why do bonds often receive an abbreviated listing?

Bonds are not as popular an investment among individual investors as stocks and when editors are considering what to include in the financial section they cut information on less-popular investments. Also, many bond investors have a relatively long investment horizon and, thus, little interest in a bond's daily price range.

Why are so many more stocks than bonds listed in the financial pages?

Bond listings are usually confined to bonds that are listed on the New York Stock Exchange and, sometimes, the American Stock Exchange. Although the number of bonds listed on these two exchanges is quite large, many bonds trade infrequently and are not included in the price listings on a daily basis. Bond transactions in the over-the-counter market are omitted from most financial publications.

How can I determine the value for a corporate bond that is traded in the over-the-counter market?

Price quotations for bonds traded in the over-the-counter market can be obtained from a broker.

How do I read the page with option listings?

Option listings represent the previous day's option closing prices as categorized by expiration date and strike
price. You may remember from an earlier chapter that
an option's strike price is the price at which the option
owner can buy stock (if the option is a call) or sell stock
(if the option is a put). Expiration dates are usually arranged across the top and expiration dates are listed down
the side of each stock's option entries. Most listings includes three expiration dates for call options and three
expiration dates for put options.

   Suppose you are interested in determining the price
for Coca Cola call options with a strike price of 60 and
an August expiration. Once you locate Coca Cola options,
scan down the strike price column to the $60 listing and
then scan to the right until you come to the column that
designates an August expiration (the date will be at the
top of the column). The quotation of 4-1/2 (for example)
indicates that at yesterday's close you could have paid
$450 (the quotation of 4-1/2 times 100 shares per option)
for a call option that would allow you to purchase 100
shares of Coca Cola until August at a fixed price of $60
per share.

If options are so popular, why don't many financial publications include option listings?

Most newspapers are unwilling to devote the considerable amount of space that is required for option listings.

Chapter 9

How Are Securities Valued?

Chapter Summary

If you are of the opinion that security prices randomly bounce up and down without rhyme nor reason, don't feel alone because some experienced investors agree with your assessment. However, most financial analysts believe that security values are influenced by a variety of variables including earnings, dividends, interest rates, inflation, and so forth, depending upon the specific kind of security being valued. This chapter discusses some of the ideas concerning security valuation.

How are securities valued?

Securities are not all alike and, thus, are not all valued in the same manner. For example, the values of U.S. Treasury bonds depend on interest payments made by the bonds and market rates of interest, while corporate bond values depend on the same two variables plus the issuer's credit quality. The valuation of stocks is much more complicated and also more subjective.

Is there a formula that can be used to calculate the exact value of a security?

Financial theory holds that the value of any investment is equal to the present value of all the cash flows that will be received by the owner(s) of the investment. Cash flows include interest payments, dividends, repayment of principal at maturity, proceeds from selling a security, and so forth. Although this part of the valuation process is relatively uncomplicated in theory, putting the idea into practice is often a problem. For example, while theory tells us that the value of a share of stock is equal to the present value of all the future dividends, it is difficult to develop accurate estimates for any given stock's future dividend payments.

Are future dividends, interest payments, and other cash flows the only considerations in valuing a security?

The second part of security valuation involves discounting projected cash flows back to the present. The need to discount stems from the fact that a given amount of cash is worth less the longer it takes to obtain the cash. The present value is calculated by discounting each of the expected cash flows by a rate that reflects the rate of interest on Treasury securities plus an added amount for the uncertain size of the cash flows. The greater the uncertainty, the larger the rate of discount. The rate of interest paid by Treasury securities changes constantly so that the rate at which a security's projected cash flows are discounted is also constantly changing.

It appears that there may be many different opinions concerning a security's value?

Variations in perceived values are especially large when substantial uncertainty surrounds an investment's future cash flows. For example, a company operating in an emerging technical field is subject to substantial hazards so that there will be a wide range of estimates concerning the true value of the firm's stock. On the other hand, bonds are relatively easy to value.

Why are bonds easier to value than stocks?

Securities are valued on the basis of all the future cash payments that will be made to owners of the securities. Bonds make fixed payments that are easily determined (unless the issuer is on shaky financial grounds) for a specific length of time. Many investments, including common stocks, make cash payments that are very difficult to accurately estimate.

If the cash payments that determine the bond's value are easy to estimate, why do I hear one expert telling investors to sell bonds at the same time that another expert is telling investors to buy bonds?

Recommendations relative to bonds are nearly always based on the experts' expectations regarding future interest rates. Experts who recommend the purchase of bonds are expecting interest rates to fall while experts who recommend that bonds be sold are expecting interest rates to increase. Although a bond's cash payments are easy to project, future interest rates are very difficult to estimate.

When a bond's cash payments are fixed how do future interest rates influence the bond's value?

Interest rate changes influence the rate at which cash flows are discounted. As interest rates rise, the rate at which a bond's cash flows are discounted increases and the present value of the cash flows (the bond's value) declines.

How do financial analysts estimate future dividends?

Financial analysts investigate a firm's financial statements (e.g., its income statement, balance sheet, cash flow statements, and so forth) and the accounting procedures that were used to produce these statements. Analysts are particularly interested in how the firm's accountants arrived at the income figure contained the income statement. The analysts may also visit the firm's facilities and interview the managers. Analysts are always looking for assets that have the potential to produce substantial amounts of additional income, but for one reason or another, are not being fully utilized. These analysts hope to uncover information that provides a reason to believe future profits and dividends will be different than the current consensus.

What do you mean by *the current consensus*?

A stock is valued on the basis of the future cash flows expected by the investment community. Financial analysts are constantly searching for stocks for which the investment community estimates are wrong. That is, financial analysts are always on the lookout for stocks that are undervalued (the investment community is underestimating future cash flows) or overvalued (the investment community is overestimating future cash flows).

Sometimes a company will announce higher earnings and the company's stock price will decline. At other times, a company will announce lower earnings and the firm's stock price will rise. What gives?

If the investment community is expecting an announcement of lower earnings there will be little surprise or excitement when lower earnings are announced. The firm's stock price will already have declined to reflect the investors' expectations of disappointing earnings. If the firm subsequently announces lower earnings, but earnings that are not as low as most investors expected, then investors will be pleasantly surprised and the stock price is likely to rise. On the other hand, if a company announces higher earnings but the increase in earnings is less than expected, then the stock might actually decline in price when the earnings announcement is made.

You're saying that investors' estimate of future cash flows has changed?

That's right. If the earnings decline is less than investors expect, then investors will revise their estimates of future cash flows upward. If the earnings increase is less than expected, then investors will revise their estimates of future cash flows downward. Each of these revisions will be reflected in changes in the stock value.

I have noticed that companies will sometimes announce lower earnings but leave dividends unchanged. Sometimes, firms will even raise dividends slightly when earnings have declined. Why?

Most companies share earnings with stockholders by paying the stockholders quarterly dividends. The quarterly dividend is more than merely sharing, however. Directors often use the dividend decision to relay information to stockholders and to the investment community at large. For example, a firm's directors may increase dividends at the same time they announce reduced earnings to let investors know that the directors consider earnings problems to be of a temporary nature. That is, the directors are telling investors to look for a reversal of the earnings decline.

Are these dividend signals generally accurate?

Not necessarily. The directors may have several motives for keeping the firm's stock price from declining. For example, the company may be considering an issue of additional stock or the directors may be concerned about a takeover attempt by another firm. Alternatively, the directors may simply be misjudging the firm's fortunes.

Why do stocks sometimes decline in price when a company makes an offer to purchase another firm?

Investors may feel that the acquiring company is paying too much for the acquisition. Buying another firm may require that the acquiring firm will have to borrow a substantial amount of money or issue a large number of new shares of its own common stock. In either case, future cash flow estimates are likely to be affected.

But if one firm purchases another company, it would seem that cash flows of the acquiring company should increase. What could cause cash flow estimates to decline and thereby result in a lower price for the stock?

The interest expense on money that is borrowed to buy the other company may be so large that analysts expect these interest expenses to penalize future cash flows. At the same time, investors may believe the new borrowing increases the riskiness of the firm. Another consideration is that a stock's value is determined by the firm's estimated cash flows divided by the number of shares of stock that are outstanding. If new shares of stock are used to pay for the acquisition, the additional shares may more than offset any increases in total cash flow resulting from the acquisition.

If dividends are so important to the value of common stocks, why are some common stocks that pay only small dividends so valuable?

Companies can choose to pay out earnings in the form of dividends or they can retain these earnings for reinvestment in the business. Hopefully, if earnings are rein-vested the new assets will allow the firm to earn even higher profits in future years. Thus, reinvestment of earn-ings permits a company to earn greater profits that, in turn, establishes a base from which to pay higher divi-dends in future years. These dividends may not be forth-coming in the next several years or even the next decade. However, at some point the additional cash flows coming into the firm will be returned to stockholders in the form of higher dividends.

Do stock prices follow trends in economic activity?

Most analysts feel that stock prices lead changes in eco-nomic activity. In other words, stock values increase prior economic upturns and stock values decline prior to the start of recessions. Remember, financial analysts are con-tinually attempting to estimate *future* cash flows. If ana-lysts are expecting a recession to begin several months in the future, the analysts will revise their cash flow estimates downward, thereby reducing the perceived value of the stock.

By the time the government announces that the economy is in a recession is it too late to sell my stock?

It is likely that by the time the economy has officially entered a recession stock prices have fully adjusted to the reduced level of economic activity. In fact, stock prices may be heading upward by that time in anticipation of an economic recovery.

Should I buy and sell stocks on the basis of public in-formation, say an unusually favorable earnings an-nouncement, or has information already been

incorporated into a stock's price by the time the information is made public?

Evidence seems to suggest that by the time information becomes public it is probably too late to profit from the information by purchasing or selling stock. In other words, by the time a firm makes a news announcement, the news has already had an impact on the firm's stock price. Even if the news is a major surprise, it will be necessary for an investor to act immediately to have a chance of taking advantage of the news. For the vast majority of investors, this kind of a reaction is impossible. The bottom line is that most individual investors have little chance of profiting through the use of public information. By the time they receive the information, it is too late to put it to good use.

I don't have the expertise to forecast a stock's future dividend payments let alone the knowledge to calculate the present value of these cash flows. How can I judge the value of a security?

You can do like the vast majority of investors and trust the judgment of others who have more expertise and more time to spend on the job of security valuation. These experts may include your broker or research analysts employed by the broker's firm who share their recommendations in company publications. There are hundreds of investment advisory services that provide investors with recommendations relative to security values.

I have a friend who uses stock price charts to choose which securities to buy and sell. How does this work?

The charting of security prices is a type of *technical analysis* of stocks. Technical analysis attempts to identify variables that will accurately forecast security prices.

Some investors use graphs of stock prices while other analysts rely on technical indicators such as trading volume, stock issues advancing versus stock issues declining, the investment quality of actively traded stocks, and so forth. The list is virtually without end.

What is the theory behind technical analysis?

Because institutional investors have the resources to make informed investment decisions, if individual investors can determine what investment decisions the institutions are making, then individuals can follow their lead and take advantage of all the work the institutions have already done. Investors who use technical analysis believe that certain stock market variables, if correctly interpreted, can provide guidance as to what informed, big-money investors are up to. That is, pension funds, investment companies, and trust departments provide clues as to which securities they are buying and selling.

What about stock price charts? How can these help?

Charts showing a stock's price history (e.g., daily, weekly, or monthly prices for many periods) can produce graphic formations that indicate buying and selling pressures from large investors. The idea is to interpret price formations and make a decision as to whether a stock should be purchased or sold.

Can these charts be used to forecast not only which direction a stock price will move, but also the extent of the movement?

Some investors who use charts feel that certain chart formations are useful in projecting price levels as well as indicating the direction of future price movements.

What kinds of information are necessary and where can the information be located?

Most chartists keep price information on a daily basis although some investors keep weekly or monthly charts. An investor keeping a daily price chart needs a stock's daily high price, daily low price, closing price, and trading volume. Each of these items can be found in *The Wall Street Journal* and in most large daily newspapers.

Once I obtain all this information how do I use it?

Most security price charts are constructed with the stock price on the vertical axis (up and down) and time on the horizontal axis (across the bottom). The price of the stock being charted determines the scale used on the vertical axis. The price range needs to be sufficiently wide that the stock can be charted over a period of months without having the price go off the scale. Each trading day, the high and low prices are marked and a straight vertical line is drawn between these two points. A small horizontal notch is used to indicate the stock's closing price on that date. This process is continued each day and, hopefully, formations will develop that will assist the investor in making investment decisions (see Appendix H).

Maintaining price charts sounds like a lot of work. Can I buy charts that have already been prepared?

There are commercial services that sell price charts. Some firms even provide price data via telephone so that investors with computers, modems, and appropriate software can download data that will construct up-to-date charts. It is still up to the individual investor to interpret the charts.

How will I know which formations are useful?

There are a number of books devoted to a discussion of technical analysis and most of these contain a large number of stock price formations that are used by technical analysts. If you find that you are interested in learning more about charting you need to visit your local library (or bookstore) and locate a book devoted to the topic of technical analysis.

What are some other technical tools?

Technical analysts pay close attention to a stock's trading volume. The thought is that if the trading in a stock becomes unusually heavy, something important will likely be occurring even if there isn't any news concerning the firm. If the stock price increases on heavy volume, then it may be time to buy the stock. The reverse logic applies if a stock price declines on heavy volume.

Other technical tools include the number of issues that decline compared to the number of issues that increase, the amount of cash being held by mutual funds, and the proportion of stock analysts who are bullish compared to the proportion who are bearish. There are hundreds of other variables that investors use in an attempt to forecast security prices.

Is it better to select stocks by using technical analysis or by using fundamental analysis?

There are professional stock analysts who swear by technical analysis and others who choose to use fundamental analysis. There are also those who believe that both methods of analysis can be useful. For example, some analysts feel that fundamental analysis should be used to determine which stocks to buy and sell while technical analysis should be used to determine when to buy and sell securities.

Chapter 10

WHAT ARE MUTUAL FUNDS?

CHAPTER SUMMARY

Mutual funds are investment companies that funnel the money of individual investors into professionally selected portfolios of securities. The funds allow individual investors who have only modest amounts of money to acquire diversified portfolios of securities. Mutual funds levy several charges that vary widely among the hundreds of available funds so that it is important for an investor to undertake some homework before committing money to a mutual fund.

What is a mutual fund?

A mutual fund is a company that invests the shareholders' money in securities. Rather than owning buildings, manufacturing equipment, and inventory, a mutual fund owns stocks or bonds or a combination of the two securities. The funds' profits are earned from increases in the value of securities that are owned plus dividends and interest that are received.

As an investor, how can I make money from owning mutual funds?

Because of certain federal regulations, mutual funds pass along virtually all dividends and interest income to stockholders. Thus, owners of mutual fund shares will earn current dividend income just like the owners of bonds and stocks receive interest and dividends. Also, investors earn capital gains and suffer capital losses as the market value of a mutual fund's shares change. The income opportunities for investors who buy mutual funds are identical to the income opportunities for investors who purchase individual security issues.

How does a mutual fund decide upon which securities to buy?

A mutual fund employs professional investment managers who decide which securities to buy and sell. The hope is that professional managers with extensive investment experience and knowledge of the securities markets can make better decisions than individual investors. Also, mutual funds invest large amounts of money which allows them to obtain favorable brokerage fees. In addition, mutual fund portfolio managers have access to sophisticated investment research to use in making investment decisions.

Does a mutual fund buy securities to hold or do the fund managers actively buy and sell securities?

Most mutual fund managers engage in active trading of the funds' securities, although trading activity varies from one fund to the next. Fund managers are constantly attempting to identify and sell securities that are overvalued and to replace these with securities that are judged to be undervalued. Mutual funds must pay brokerage commissions to buy and sell securities, but the size of trades are quite large and the fees on a per share basis are relatively low compared to the fees that individual investors must pay.

Do all mutual funds have similar security portfolios?

Mutual funds can be categorized depending on the kinds of securities they own. For example, some mutual funds invest only in stocks while other mutual funds limit their holdings to bonds. These categories are further subdivided and many mutual funds that limit their holdings specialize in particular types of stocks. Some funds buy stocks that pay high dividends while other funds limit their holdings to stocks that have a potential for large price appreciation. Some mutual funds even limit their holdings to the securities of foreign issuers.

Do mutual funds that own bonds also specialize?

Mutual funds that limit their holdings to bonds also specialize, but to a lesser extent than funds that buy stocks. For example, some funds buy only bonds that pay tax-exempt interest and a few funds even specialize in tax-exempt bonds from a particular state. Some bond funds specialize in bonds of a particular maturity length. For example, one fund might own only bonds with long maturities while another fund might specialize in bonds with intermediate maturities.

Do any mutual funds own both bonds and stocks?

Some mutual funds, called *balanced funds*, own both stocks and bonds. Balanced funds are considered "middle-of-the-road" funds that offer the potential of capital growth at the same time that current income is earned. Owning a balanced fund would produce much the combined effect as investing both in a fund that specializes in stocks and a fund that specializes in bonds.

How can I purchase shares of a mutual fund?

Mutual funds are sold directly by the sponsors and through a variety of financial institutions such as broker-age firms. To purchase shares directly, an individual must phone or write the sponsor (see Appendix R).

Can mutual fund shares be transferred to other investors or are shareholders required to wait until a certain maturity date when shares are redeemed?

Mutual funds are unique in that the sponsors stand ready to repurchase their own shares (see Appendix S). A mutual fund shareholder who wishes to liquidate all or a portion of an investment can request that the sponsor redeem the shares. Mutual fund shares, like common stocks, have no maturity date.

What price will I receive when I sell shares of a mutual fund?

Unless a fee is involved in the sale, for each share you sell you will receive the fund's *net asset value* (NAV)—an amount equal to the value of all the securities owned by the fund divided by the number of the fund's shares that are outstanding. For example, if the fund owns $105 million worth of securities (valued at current prices) and has 20 million shares of its own stock outstanding, you should receive $5.25 ($105 million/20 million shares) for each share that you sell.

Can I purchase additional shares of a mutual fund?

Mutual funds are structured such that new shares of stock are always available for sale. Shares may be purchased by current owners or by individuals who are acquiring the fund's shares for the first time. For example, you can purchase 100 shares of the fund today and then buy another 50 shares several months later. The price that you pay for the additional shares may be more or less than the price you paid for the original shares.

Will I pay the net asset value when I buy additional shares?

When you purchase shares in the fund you will pay the net asset value in effect at the time of your purchase. Some funds also charge a sales fee that is added to the net asset value. The net asset value of the fund's shares will change as the value of securities held by the fund change. If securities owned by the fund increase in value there will be an increase in the net asset value of the fund's own shares. If securities owned by the fund decline in value there will be a decrease in the net asset value of the fund's shares.

So, the value of my shares in the fund are directly affected by the value of the securities that are owned by the fund?

The value of your shares will vary directly with the combined values of the securities that are held by the fund. If the fund's portfolio manager invests wisely, you will benefit from gains in the value of your shares. In fact, one of the two major benefits on which mutual funds are sold is that average investors who own mutual funds are able to take advantage of the investment expertise of professional money managers. If this expertise proves effective, the fund's shareholders should earn higher returns than if the investors made their own investment decisions.

Do the market values of mutual fund shares move up and down very much?

The volatility of a mutual fund's shares depends entirely upon the price volatility of the securities owned by the fund. If a mutual fund owns securities that are subject to large price movements, the fund's shares will be subject to large changes in value. However, a mutual fund's shares tend to be less volatile than the prices of most of the individual stocks that are owned by the fund because price movements in some stocks will tend to cancel out some of the price movements of other stocks held by the fund.

Is share price volatility of a mutual fund important?

The importance of the volatility of a mutual fund's shares depends upon the goals of the investor. If an investor anticipates there may be a need to sell the shares on short notice, then price volatility can be very important. On the other hand, if an investor looks at the long-term and anticipates being able to ride out short-term price changes, price volatility may be relatively unimportant.

You mentioned that expert money management is one of two benefits from investing in mutual funds. What is the other benefit?

A major benefit from investing in mutual funds is the instant diversification that is achieved. Individual investors cannot hope to assemble a diversified portfolio of securities without having a large amount of investment capital. Mutual funds allow investors who have only nominal amounts of money to achieve immediate diversification.

Are certain mutual funds more diversified than other mutual funds?

During the 1980s, investors became increasingly interested in mutual funds with specialized portfolios. For example, a mutual fund might specialize in the stocks of high-technology companies or in stocks issued within a certain foreign country or a within a certain geographic region. Mutual funds with specialized portfolios offer substantially less diversification than funds that do not have specialized portfolios.

What kinds of fees are involved when investing in mutual funds?

Several kinds of fees are charged by mutual funds although not all mutual funds charge the same kinds or the same size fees. In fact, fee structures can be quite different among the hundreds of mutual funds that are sold to investors.

One fee that all funds have in common is an annual management fee designed to pay the portfolio managers and cover the fund's operating expenses. This annual fee generally ranges between one-half of one percent and slightly over one percent of a fund's assets. For example, a mutual fund with $100 million in assets and a management fee of one percent will levy an annual management fee of $1 million. The dollar amount of the fee (but not the percentage) will increase as the fund grows in size. The percentage size of the fee frequently declines as the size of the fund increases.

How can I determine the size of a fund's management fee?

All of a fund's fees are spelled out in the prospectus that can be obtained from the fund or from the fund's salesperson. You should carefully read the prospectus and examine the fees charged by the fund.

What other kinds of fees are charged?

Mutual funds sold by brokers and other salespeople generally levy a fee either when an investor purchases shares or when shares are redeemed. These fees can amount to as much as 8-1/2 percent of the money invested although the size of the fee is subject to substantial variation from one fund to the next. The mutual fund's prospectus will spell out any sales fee as well as the management fee.

How is a fee applied when shares are redeemed?

Some mutual funds charge a redemption fee or "exit fee" when shares are sold. Often, these firms levy a percentage fee that is reduced the longer that shares have been held. For example, a fund might have an exit fee of six percent of the sales price if shares have been held a year or less, a fee of five percent if shares have been held between one and two years, and so forth. If shares have been held five or six years, there may be no redemption fee. Again, any redemption fee should be explained in the mutual fund's prospectus.

Can you provide an example of how an exit fee works?

Suppose three years ago you purchased 300 shares of a mutual fund at a price of $15 per share. No sales fee was levied at the time of purchase, although the prospectus indicated the firm charged an annual management fee of 0.75 percent of the fund's assets and levied a redemption fee equal to four percent of the net asset value of the fund's shares at the time of redemption. If you sell all 300 shares for $50 each, you will pay a redemption fee of $600 (four percent of $15,000). The redemption fee will be taken out before you receive the proceeds of the sale.

Are there any other fees?

Some mutual funds levy what is termed a 12b-1 fee. This is an annual percentage that is charged against the market value of the fund. Although the 12b-1 fee is similar to the annual management fee discussed earlier, proceeds from the 12b-1 fee are utilized to cover the fund's marketing expenses rather than its management costs. Essentially, a 12b-1 fee is a charge against current shareholders to pay for recruiting additional shareholders.

Are there mutual funds that don't charge any fees?

There are mutual funds that don't charge any initial sales fees, exit fees, or 12b-1 fees. However, all funds levy a management fee that covers the funds' operating expenses. Somebody has to pay for the costs of running the fund.

If there are funds that don't charge sales or redemption fees, is there a reason to purchase mutual funds that do charge a fee?

Many financial planners advise investors to limit choices to mutual funds that levy only a management fee. However, an important consideration is the degree of assistance you need in selecting a fund. Many individual investors do not have the expertise to make an informed selection from among the hundreds and hundreds of funds that are sold. Do you want to own a stock fund, a bond fund, or a balanced fund? If you decide upon a stock fund, do you want a fund that specializes in growth stocks, in income stocks, or in stocks of Pacific Rim companies? The alternatives are virtually endless and decisions are not made easily.

With the large number of funds that are available, how do I decide which fund to buy?

You must first decide what it is you want to accomplish by owning shares of a mutual fund. For example, are you after current income or capital appreciation? If you are seeking current income, how much risk are you willing to accept? If you seek current income but are unwilling to assume much risk, then you may want to consider mutual funds that invest in high-grade corporate bonds or U.S. Treasury securities.

After I determine my investment goals, won't there still be hundreds of funds to choose from?

There are numerous funds within virtually every category of funds so you will need to narrow your choices among funds with similar goals. You may want to look at a fund's intermediate-term and long-term track record and to investigate the fees charged by each fund. Several publications including *Money*, *Forbes*, and *Business Week* list the fees and historical investment performance of individual funds. Some publications award a rating to each fund on the basis of the fund's relative investment performance.

Are mutual funds traded on the New York Stock Exchange?

There is no secondary market for mutual fund shares so that funds are not listed on the New York Stock Exchange or on any other stock exchange. Mutual fund shares are purchased directly from the sponsor and sold directly to the sponsor.

How can I check on the value of a mutual fund?

Mutual fund quotations are published daily in *The Wall Street Journal* and in some metropolitan newspapers. Other newspapers publish weekly quotations in the Saturday or Sunday edition. *The Wall Street Journal* publishes both the net asset value and the offering price for each fund. If a mutual fund does not levy a sales charge the offering price and net asset value will be the same. Nearly all funds have a toll-free telephone number that permits investors to inquire about share prices.

I read that there are similar investments to mutual funds that can be bought at a discount. What are these investments?

Mutual funds are one kind of investment company. Another less-popular kind of investment company is the closed-end investment company. Closed-end investment companies are organized in an identical manner to other corporations. That is, a closed-end investment company is organized with a specific number of shares of stock. These shares are sold to investors and no further shares are issued except in rare instances. Also, the investment company will not redeem its outstanding shares.

How does a shareholder liquidate the shares?

Shares in closed-end investment companies are traded in an identical manner to shares in other corporations. Some closed-end shares are traded on the exchanges and other closed-end investment company shares are traded in the over-the-counter market. Investors who wish to liquidate these shares must sell the shares in the open market. Share prices may be above, below, or equal to the stock's net asset value. Thus, shares in closed-end investment companies can often be purchased at a discount from the net asset value.

Isn't this a good deal?

It depends. You may purchase shares at a discount to net asset value and later find that you must sell the shares at an even greater discount to net asset value. On the other hand, who is to say that the shares may not move from a discount to a premium to net asset value?

Why do these discounts and premiums to net asset value exist?

No one seems to have a very good answer to this question although many individuals have spent a lot of time trying to come up with some reasonable explanations.

Should I buy shares in a mutual fund?

Buying mutual fund shares is a good introduction to investing in securities. An investor can take advantage of diversification and professional expertise at the same time that investment experience is gained. If you do decide to invest in mutual funds be sure that you understand the fees you will be charged and that you choose a fund with investment goals that are compatible with your personal goals.

Chapter 11

HOW ARE WALL STREET INVESTMENTS AFFECTED BY TAXES?

CHAPTER SUMMARY

Investors should make financial decisions based upon after-tax returns that the investments are expected to produce. Taxes are a fact of life that apply to investments sold by Wall Street as well as investments sold by your local bank or savings and loan association. Investors must pay taxes on dividends and most interest payments that are received, in addition to incurring tax liabilities on gains from the sale of securities. This chapter discusses some of the important tax questions that investors will face when they invest in Wall Street.

Will I be able to avoid taxes by investing in Wall Street?

With isolated exceptions, Wall Street investments produce taxable income. Of course, if your Wall Street investments lose value you may actually save on taxes as you use these losses to offset other income. However, investing to produce losses in order to save taxes is not a goal of most investors.

If I can't avoid taxes, why should I invest in Wall Street?

Wall Street offers the opportunity to acquire a diversified group of investment assets that can provide protection from some of the risks that will be discussed in the next chapter. Also, Wall Street investments may provide an opportunity to earn higher rates of return compared to the rates that are offered by certificates of deposit, savings accounts, and insurance policies.

What kinds of taxes will I be required to pay on Wall Street investments?

If you purchase shares of stock—either common stocks or preferred stocks—you will be required to pay taxes on any dividends that you receive. Dividends are taxable at the same rate as wages and salaries. If you purchase corporate bonds or U.S. government bonds you will be required to pay taxes on the interest you receive. Like dividends, interest income is taxed at the same rate as income earned from wages.

How does the Internal Revenue Service know that I receive dividends and interest?

Organizations that pay dividends and interest are required to report annually the amounts you were paid during the year to both you and the Internal Revenue Service. The Internal Revenue Service requires that you report the amounts of income that are listed on these forms. If the reporting on your income tax return doesn't agree with information that has been sent to the IRS you can expect a letter requesting an explanation.

Will dividend and interest payments be subject to withholding?

Most investors will not be subject to withholding on dividends and interest, although it will be necessary for the investor to sign a form confirming that withholding is not required. Several years ago, the federal government attempted to initiate withholding on dividends and interest, but a public outcry ensued (sponsored primarily by commercial banks) and the proposal was rescinded.

I have heard that some interest is not taxable. Is this incorrect?

Most interest from the bonds issued by state and local governments is not taxable as income by the federal government and may not be taxable by the state and local governments where you reside. For example, if you are a resident of Georgia and purchase a bond issued by the city of Valdosta, Georgia, you will not have to pay either federal or state income taxes on interest income from the bond. Policy varies from state to state with respect to how municipal bond interest is taxed.

Why doesn't everyone buy municipal bonds?

Tax-exempt municipal bonds are so desirable that these bonds don't need to pay a very high rate of interest in order to attract buyers (see Appendix U). For example, at the same time that General Motors might have to pay an interest rate of ten percent to sell an issue of bonds, the city of Detroit may be able to issue tax-exempt bonds with an interest rate of only seven percent. Some investors find that the tax exemption for interest income does not offset the low interest rate on a security with tax-exempt interest payments.

What determines whether an investor should purchase municipal bonds?

The decision to purchase municipal bonds hinges on whether the municipal bonds produce a higher after-tax return compared to the return available on taxable bonds (see Appendix T). Municipal bonds are more likely to be a good investment choice depending on the greater the investor's tax rate, and the smaller the difference between interest rates on taxable bonds and interest rates on municipal bonds. In general, only investors with substantial amounts of taxable income should consider buying municipal bonds.

Is interest on U.S. government obligations taxable?

Interest on Treasury securities is taxable by the federal government but is not taxable by state and local governments. If you reside in a state that levies a high tax on personal income, ownership of federal obligations can produce important tax savings although the savings doesn't approach the reduction in federal taxes that results from owning municipal bonds.

What other taxes have an impact on Wall Street investors?

Gains and losses that are realized when securities are sold will have an impact on an investor's taxes. When securities are sold for more than their cost, the gain (but not the total proceeds of the sale) becomes taxable income. When securities are sold for less than their cost, the loss can be used to offset other income so that it reduces taxable income.

Are taxes due on appreciation in the value of a security that occurs while I am holding the security?

Appreciation must be realized through a sale before a gain is taxed. So long as a security continues to be held no tax will be due on any price appreciation. The same rule applies to losses. If a security declines in value following the date of purchase you will be unable to utilize the loss to reduce your taxable income unless you sell the security.

Can you provide an example of how a gain is calculated?

If you purchase 100 shares of IBM common stock at a price of $105 per share and pay a brokerage commission of $150, your cost basis for the shares equals the principal amount of the trade (100 × $105, or $10,500) plus the $150 commission, or $10,650. If you later sell the stock at a price of $130 per share and pay a brokerage commission of $175, the net proceeds equal the principal amount of the sale (100 × $130, or $13,000) less the $175 commission, or $12,825. Taxable income from the sale is $2,175, the difference between $12,825 in proceeds and your $10,650 cost basis. You will be required to report $2,175 in additional income on your next tax return.

Will the entire gain of $2,175 be taxable?

The entire amount of a gain is taxable although the rate of taxation may be slightly lower than the rate that is applied to other income.

Why would the tax rate be slightly lower than the rate that is applicable to my other income?

At the time this is written, there are three federal tax rates applied to individual income. For married couples filing joint returns, the rates are 15 percent on the first $32,450 of taxable income, 28 percent on taxable income between $32,450 and $78,400, and 31 percent on all taxable income over $78,400. The same three rates apply to unmarried individuals and heads of households, although the income brackets are different (see Appendix V).

The federal government applies a maximum tax rate of 28 percent to capital gains. Thus, a couple with sufficient income to pay taxes at a rate of up to 31 percent on their regular income will pay a rate of only 28 percent on gains from the sale of stocks, bonds, and other capital assets.

No matter how much in gains I earn from the sale of stocks and bonds, I will not be taxed at a rate of more than 28 percent?

With the tax rates currently in effect, the maximum federal tax rate on capital gains is 28 percent. Of course, tax rates are subject to change, so there is no guarantee that the maximum rate on capital gains will remain at 28 percent.

If I buy securities when the maximum tax rate on capital gains is 28 percent, will the 28-percent rate apply to the sale of these securities even though tax rates have subsequently been changed by the time I sell the securities?

The chances are that you will be required to pay the tax rate in effect at the time you sell the securities, not the rate that was in effect at the time you acquired the securities. Not knowing the rate of taxation that will be applicable to an investment introduces a degree of uncertainty into investing.

If my income from wages and dividends is relatively small, and I currently pay a federal tax rate of only 15 percent, will capital gains that I realize still be taxed at a rate of 28 percent?

No. Only a maximum tax rate is specified for capital gains. Otherwise, capital gains are added to other income and taxed at whatever rate is appropriate for the investor's total income. If annual income produced by wages, interest, and capital gains is small enough to fall into the 15-percent tax bracket, then the capital gains will only be taxed at a rate of 15 percent unless the gains are so large an amount they place you in the next higher tax bracket.

What if I sell several different securities during the same year and some of the sales produce gains while other sales produce losses?

Gains and losses that are realized during the same year offset one another. Suppose during a year you sell three securities, one for a loss of $3,000 and two for gains of $2,000 and $5,000, respectively. The loss offsets $3,000 of the total gains of $7,000, leaving a $4,000 net gain. Only the net gain of $4,000 is taxable.

What if the total realized losses exceed the total realized gains for the year?

The same rule applies here. That is, you consolidate all of your gains and losses. If this produces a net loss, the loss is used to reduce your taxable income. However, net losses can only be utilized to a maximum of $3,000 per year. Net losses above $3,000 must be carried over to future years where they can be used to offset future gains and to reduce taxable income in those years.

If I have a large amount of realized gains, will I be required to report all of the net gain even though I am only able to utilize $3,000 in net losses per year?

That is correct. There is a limit on the amount of realized losses that can be used to reduce taxable income but there is no limit on the amount of realized gains that are taxable in the year the gains are realized.

Am I required to pay taxes on a realized gain from a municipal bond?

Even though most municipal bonds pay tax-exempt interest, you will be required to pay taxes on any gains that are realized from owning the municipal bonds.

Is there any way that I can keep from paying a tax on capital gains?

As mentioned previously, you can avoid taxation by simply not selling the security. The problem is that until you sell a stock or bond, you can't get your money out of the security unless you take out a loan that uses the security as collateral. If you hold an appreciated security until your death, your heirs will inherit the security at the market value on the date of your death. This means that any gain that occurred during the time you held the security will be lost forever for tax purposes. Unfortunately, you must die to obtain this tax benefit.

On a more positive note, you can make charitable contributions using appreciated securities and avoid the payment of capital gains taxes. In fact, you are able to deduct the value of the securities at the time of the gift rather than deduct only your cost basis on the securities. Donating appreciated securities is a popular method for wealthy individuals to make charitable contributions at minimal cost.

If I purchase a zero-coupon bond at a very large discount from face value, will I be able to defer taxes either until I sell the bond or until the bond matures?

Most bonds that are bought at huge discounts from face value will require the payment of taxes each year the bonds are owned, even though no interest payments are received by the owners. Zero-coupon bonds create a cash flow problem for most investors because owners of these bonds must pay taxes even though no interest payments are being received to help make the payments.

If no interest payments are made, how will the Internal Revenue Service know that I should be reporting this interest?

The issuer will send identical 1099 forms to you and to the Internal Revenue Service each year showing the amount of interest that "accrued" on the bond.

How is income from mutual funds taxed?

Income from mutual funds is taxed in the same manner as income from securities. Mutual funds that own stocks and corporate bonds pay dividends that the mutual fund stockholders must report as taxable income. Likewise, mutual funds sometimes sell securities at a gain and make distributions of capital gains to stockholders who must report and pay taxes on the gains. Mutual funds that invest in municipal bonds pass through tax-exempt interest payments that do not have to be reported as taxable income.

What about changes in the value of mutual fund shares that I own?

Changes in the value of mutual fund shares are treated in the same manner as other securities. That is, any gain that is realized from the sale of mutual fund shares must be reported as a capital gain and included in taxable income. Likewise, realized losses from mutual fund ownership reduce taxable income. Gains and losses on mutual fund shares have no effect on taxable income until shares are sold and gains and losses are realized.

If I borrow money to finance my investments, will I be permitted to use the interest on my loan as a deduction on my tax return?

Interest expense is deductible so long as the borrowed funds are used to produce investment income. Thus, if you borrow money to buy shares of stock, you may use the interest cost on the borrowed funds to offset dividend income that you earn from the stock. An exception is that you may not deduct the interest on a loan that is used to acquire tax-exempt municipal bonds.

Can I deduct interest that is used to buy Treasury securities?

Yes, you may deduct interest on loans to buy Treasury securities.

Do I have to borrow the money from my broker in order to use the interest as a deduction?

It doesn't matter where you borrow the money so long as the proceeds from the loan are used to finance income-producing investments.

Can I deduct other expenses involved in earning investment income? For example, can I deduct the cost of a subscription to *The Wall Street Journal* or the cost maintaining a brokerage account?

Most investment-related expenses may be used to reduce taxable income only when you itemize deductions rather than use the standard deduction in calculating your income tax liability. Investment expenses fall into a category of deductions called miscellaneous deductions. These expenses are permitted as itemized deductions only to the extent that they exceed two percent of your adjusted gross income.

Are investment plans, such as IRAs and Keogh plans that defer taxes until my retirement, a good deal?

Individual Retirement Accounts (IRAs), Keogh plans (for the self-employed), and other tax deferred investment plans are advantageous for several reasons. For one, the plans permit you to accumulate a larger retirement nest egg because your investment returns compound without taxes being taken out. This means that you will end up with a greater amount of money at retirement. Another advantage of tax-deferred retirement plans is that most participants hesitate to make withdrawals from the plans. Thus, the plans help insure that funds will be there for your retirement.

Are there any negative aspects to the plans?

You should be aware that all of the dollars you eventually withdraw from the fund will be taxable at the time of the withdrawal. If you decide to withdraw funds prior to your retirement, you are likely to be socked with a ten-percent penalty in addition to the tax liability on the withdrawn funds.

Another consideration to tax deferred retirement plans is the inability to know if the tax rate at the time of your retirement will be higher or lower than the tax rate that is applicable to your income at the time contributions to the plan are being made. Thus, it is possible that participating in one of these plans will defer taxes that would have been levied at a rate of 28 percent of income to some date in the future when the tax may be considerably higher than 28 percent. There is no way to know for certain what the tax rate will be when you make your withdrawals.

Chapter 12

What Are the Risks of Investing in Wall Street?

Chapter Summary

Wall Street carries substantial risks for uninformed and unsuspecting investors. Individuals who hear friends' stories about making big profits from Wall Street investments (the stories are occasionally factual) may be prone to redeploy their own savings without understanding the risks that are involved in owning securities. This chapter answers some questions concerning risk that every investor should ask.

Is investing in Wall Street more risky than purchasing certificates of deposit at my local bank or savings and loan?

Probably, but the investments peddled by Wall Street are so diverse that it is necessary to specify the type of investment you are comparing with certificates of deposit. Also, it is important to understand that there are several different risks involved in owning nearly any investment asset and some of these risks apply to owning certificates of deposit as well as to holding investment vehicles that are marketed by Wall Street firms.

What is there to risk other than the possibility of losing the money that you invest?

Risk is the uncertainty of the expected rate of return to be earned from owning an investment. The greater the uncertainty of the expected return, the greater the risk of owning the investment.

A more comprehensive view of risk is the effect of owning an asset on the riskiness of your existing investment portfolio. In other words, an investment's riskiness should be viewed from the perspective of how ownership of the asset affects the variability of the returns from all of your assets taken as a whole. It is misleading to consider the risk and return to be earned from investing in a particular asset without considering how that asset will affect the risk and return from your entire portfolio.

This is confusing. Can you give provide an example?

Most experts concede that ownership of real estate entails substantially more risk than investing in insured certificates of deposit. Real estate is often difficult to resell and may be subject to wide variations in value. Despite these negatives, an investor might actually reduce the risk of an investment portfolio by adding a real estate investment to the other assets that are owned, especially if the portfolio is heavily weighted with financial assets.

I still don't understand. How can adding a risky asset to a low-risk portfolio reduce the portfolio's riskiness?

One of the important risks faced by an investor is the potential loss of purchasing power that can result from unexpected inflation. Inflation can absolutely devastate the real value of what is generally considered a low-risk portfolio. For example, the real value of both principal and interest income produced by long-term Treasury bonds are subject to being seriously depleted by inflation.

Thus, the real returns from a portfolio that is heavily weighted with Treasury securities are subject to substantial uncertainty. The addition of tangible assets—precious metals, investment-grade coins or stamps, or real estate—helps protect such a portfolio from this type of loss.

But isn't the possibility of a reduction in value the major risk of investing?

Loss of value is an important risk to be faced by investors, but there are other considerations to risk. A major risk faced by investors who devote a heavy proportion of their portfolio to a money market fund is the possibility of a large reduction in income caused by a fall in market interest rates. For an investor who supports a major part of consumption spending from a money market fund's interest payments, the possibility of lower interest rates is a very real risk. A money market fund has a stable market value and yet an over-reliance on this particular investment places the investor at substantial risk.

What other risks are faced by Wall Street investors?

Chapter 3 discussed the importance of market rates of interest to owners of long-term bonds. If you purchase a long-term bond and market rates of interest subsequently increase, the market value of your bond will decline. The bigger the change in interest rates and the longer the maturity of your bond, the greater the change that will occur in the value of a bond. Changes in market rates of interest are a major risk faced by most investors including individuals who purchase stocks.

How are owners of common stocks affected by changes in interest rates?

Rising interest rates exert a downward pressure on stock prices. Stocks must compete for investment dollars with bonds and if both newly issued and existing bonds offer higher interest rates, investors will demand greater returns from stocks. Unless there is an increase in expected dividend streams, stocks can only offer higher returns if the market values of the stocks decline.

Do falling interest rates benefit the owners of both bonds and stocks?

Falling interest rates will tend to boost the market values of both stocks and bonds. Declining interest rates during the 1980s were accompanied by major bull markets in both stocks and bonds. Remember, however, that falling interest rates result in reduced interest income for investors who have a large proportion of their portfolios in money market accounts and short-term certificates of deposit.

If low interest rates are good for the stock and bond markets, why doesn't the government keep interest rates low?

Pushing interest rates too low for too long requires ever-bigger increases in credit expansion that eventually lead to inflationary pressures. Rising inflationary expectations will then make it even more difficult for the Federal Reserve to successfully pursue a policy promoting lower interest rates because creditors expecting higher inflation will demand a higher return from borrowers.

What other risks are faced by investors in Wall Street?

One risk is a potential difficulty in converting an investment into cash at a reasonable price. In simple terms, some investments are difficult to resell. The lack of active secondary markets results in a large spread between the price at which investments can be purchased and the price at which these same investments can be sold. Tangible assets often have large spreads between the bid and ask prices. At the opposite extreme, Treasury securities and actively traded stocks have very low spreads between bid and ask prices.

Are tangible assets the only investments that are difficult to sell?

Inactive stocks and bonds often have relatively large price spreads compared to securities with active markets. A lack of liquidity may not be particularly important to an individual who has a long investment horizon. Investors who intend to hold stocks for many years or who plan to hold bonds until maturity face little risk from owning assets that lack an active secondary market. For someone who may be required to sell on short notice, however, lack of liquidity is a substantial risk that must be taken into account when investments are selected.

What about variations in the value of an investment?

Investments that are subject to substantial variations in market value can subject some investors to significant risks. As with an investment with little liquidity, an asset that fluctuates in value presents the greatest risk to an investor who may be required to sell the investment on short notice. Substantial variations in market value are not a great risk to investors who expect a long holding period.

What kinds of investments are subject to major price variations?

Tangible assets and many common stock issues are subject to large variations in value although some stocks vary substantially more in value than do other stocks. A look at historical price charts will provide you with some idea of a stock's price volatility. Preferred stocks and long-term bonds also vary in value but not to the extent of common stocks. Investments with little variation in value include Treasury bills and other short-term debt securities. Money market funds, money market accounts, savings accounts, and short-term certificates of deposit exhibit virtually no changes in market value.

Should I favor investments with stable values?

At least a portion of your investment portfolio should be comprised of assets that have relatively stable values and excellent liquidity. Virtually all investors face the possibility of unexpected expenses that will necessitate liquidating some investments. The problem with investments having stable values is they tend to produce relatively low rates of return. Thus, keeping a large proportion of a portfolio's assets in liquid investments requires that you surrender substantial income.

What about the possibility of a security issuer going out of business or halting the payment of dividends and interest?

The possibility of a decreased income stream is a serious risk faced by investors in many Wall Street products. The risk is especially great for investors who purchase common stocks. Although businesses prefer not to reduce the dividends paid to their stockholders, reduced earnings sometime necessitate that dividends be reduced or eliminated altogether. A reduction in payments to bondholders is less likely because interest payments and principal repayment are legal obligations of the issuer.

If there is less possibility of a reduction in interest on bonds compared to a reduction in dividends on

stocks, why don't investors always prefer bonds to stocks?

Although bond interest payments are almost never decreased, bond payments are also never increased. On the other hand, while dividend payments are sometimes reduced or eliminated, dividends are often increased. The stability of payments to bondholders can be both an advantage and a disadvantage.

Is the stability of interest payments the reason that bonds provide no protection against inflation?

Bonds protect an investor against expected losses in purchasing power because expected inflation is built into the interest rate that will be earned from owning a bond. It is unexpected inflation that causes pain for bondholders (see Appendix W). An investor who owns a nine-percent coupon bond that is issued when inflation is expected be six percent anticipates a real return of three percent (before taxes). If inflation subsequently turns out to be ten-percent rate during the period the bond is owned, the investor will earn a real return that is negative.

If a company goes out of business am I better off being a bondholder or being a stockholder?

If a company goes out of business you are almost surely better off being a bondholder than a stockholder. In general, claims by bondholders are paid prior to claims by stockholders. In practice, bondholders may not recover in full because the firm may not have enough assets to pay all of the outstanding claims against it. An investor should be aware that there are often substantial differences in the priority of claims among creditors (which include bondholders) of the same firm.

Other than the varying income stream caused by changing market rates of interest, is there any risk to owning a money market fund?

First, it is important to differentiate money market deposit accounts offered by banks and savings and loans from money market funds offered by Wall Street firms. Deposit accounts at banks and S&Ls generally qualify for FDIC insurance and are free of credit risk. Money market funds offered by brokerage firms are mutual funds that invest in high-grade short-term securities. Money market funds are generally very safe investments but they are not insured. Because most money market funds invest a portion of their funds in the short-term securities of corporations there is always a possibility that some of these securities may lose substantial value because of a corporate default. Unless a fund's sponsor is willing to absorb the loss and reimburse the fund, owners of the fund's shares will find the value of their investment has declined.

What about money market funds that invest in Treasury securities?

Money market funds that limit their investments to U.S. Treasury securities do not subject investors to the possibility of a default in the fund's investments. Money market funds that invest in Treasury securities are considered to be safer than money market funds that invest in short-term corporate securities. The yields on Treasury-only funds are somewhat lower than the yields on regular money market funds, but this difference may be more than offset by the exemption of interest paid by Treasury-only funds from state and local taxes.

Why would money market funds invest in securities in which there is some possibility of default?

A fund's managers may feel that the higher yields on particular securities are worth the increased risk. Many investors paint all money market funds with the same brush by assuming that all funds are of equivalent risk. For these investors risk variations among the funds are not an issue so the investors seek out the highest yields. Don't let yourself fall into this trap.

Can I invest in Wall Street and still guard against risk?

There are several points you should always keep in mind when investing. First, never invest your money in something that you do not understand. If an investment is so complicated that you are unable to get a handle on what the investment is all about, you should avoid the investment. Many investors get burned by acquiring things they don't understand.

Another good rule is to understand why you are investing and then go about acquiring investments that fit your needs. Accomplishing this bit of investing wizardry requires that you understand the characteristics of stocks, bonds, convertible bonds, and all of the other Wall Street investments you may be considering. Investors often get into difficulty by acquiring investments that are inappropriate for their needs.

Anything else?

No matter how strongly you feel about the advantages of investing in a particular security or even a particular class of security (e.g., common stock, municipal bonds, and so forth) don't give in to the temptation of putting all of your eggs into a single basket. Even sure things occasionally turn sour. One of the keys to risk reduction is diversification. You should never invest only in stocks, only in bonds, or only in real estate. It is also generally unwise to sock away all of your funds in investments such as a money market account or Treasury securities with high liquidity and little credit risk.

Any other ideas on keeping my losses down?

Investors often lose substantial amounts of money because they become greedy. We all hear stories about certain investments being sure things and become tempted to plunge into risky investments we would ordinarily avoid. Even experienced investors who have substantial knowledge of the ways of Wall Street sometimes become greedy and chase "the big score."

Does this mean that I should not invest all of my money in Wall Street?

There is nothing wrong with keeping a portion of your portfolio in insured certificates of deposit or in a bank money market account. You may want to adjust the composition of your portfolio depending upon the returns that are available in each of the various investments.

I've read that individuals should invest in Wall Street only with funds they can afford to lose. Is this good advice?

Not necessarily. A person who desires a steady stream of cash income will find that high-grade corporate bonds and Treasury securities offered by Wall Street are excellent choices. Each of these investments involves little risk of nonpayment and each is a good substitute for certificates of deposit. Blue chip stocks have more price volatility and involve the possibility of dividend reductions but these securities also offer an opportunity to receive a stream of income that increases over time.

Does the advice of investing only the funds that I can afford to lose ever apply?

You should limit your investments to blue chip stocks, investment-grade bonds, or other low-risk assets when you use money that you cannot afford to lose. This means that you should avoid warrants, options, and the multitude of limited partnerships offered by Wall Street unless you can afford to lose a substantial portion of your funds. Avoid investing in a security that has been recommended by a friend who has it on good authority that the stock will double by Christmas.

Any last word of advice?

Take everything you read or hear about investing with a grain of salt.

Does this apply to the information contained in this book?

You will have to be the judge of that, but don't call me collect.

Appendices

Appendix A
New Issues of Securities, 1971–1990

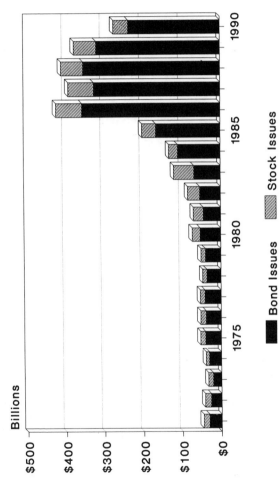

Billions

■ Bond Issues ▨ Stock Issues

1990 stock issues eliminated.

Appendix B
Public Announcement of Common Stock Issue

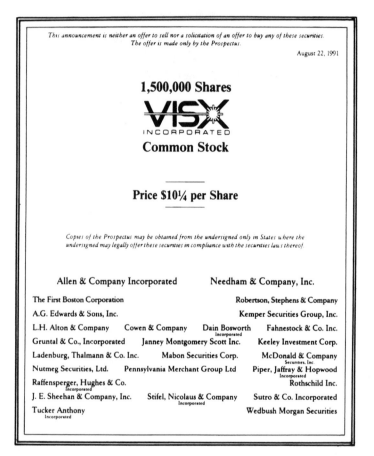

This announcement is neither an offer to sell nor a solicitation of an offer to buy any of these securities. The offer is made only by the Prospectus.

August 22, 1991

1,500,000 Shares

VISX
INCORPORATED

Common Stock

Price $10¼ per Share

Copies of the Prospectus may be obtained from the undersigned only in States where the undersigned may legally offer these securities in compliance with the securities laws thereof.

Allen & Company Incorporated   Needham & Company, Inc.

The First Boston Corporation

Robertson, Stephens & Company

A.G. Edwards & Sons, Inc.

Kemper Securities Group, Inc.

L.H. Alton & Company   Cowen & Company   Dain Bosworth Incorporated   Fahnestock & Co. Inc.

Gruntal & Co., Incorporated   Janney Montgomery Scott Inc.   Keeley Investment Corp.

Ladenburg, Thalmann & Co. Inc.   Mabon Securities Corp.   McDonald & Company Securities, Inc.

Nutmeg Securities, Ltd.   Pennsylvania Merchant Group Ltd   Piper, Jaffray & Hopwood Incorporated

Raffensperger, Hughes & Co. Incorporated   Rothschild Inc.

J. E. Sheehan & Company, Inc.   Stifel, Nicolaus & Company Incorporated   Sutro & Co. Incorporated

Tucker Anthony Incorporated   Wedbush Morgan Securities

Appendix C
Selected 1990 Financial Statistics for Several Large U.S. Firms

Company	Assets (millions)	Revenues (millions)	Net Income (millions)	L.T. Debt (millions)	Shares Outstanding (thousands)	Earnings Per Share	Dividends Per Share
AT&T	$47,775	$37,285	$2,735	$9,118	1,092,143	$2.51	$1.29
Boeing	14,591	27,595	1,385	311	343,573	4.01	.95
CBS	4,692	3,261	92	712	23,685	3.55	4.40
Coca Cola	9,278	10,236	1,382	536	668,239	2.04	.80
Dow Chemical	23,953	19,773	1,384	5,209	269,990	5.10	2.60
Eastman Kodak	24,125	18,908	703	6,989	324,638	2.17	2.00
Exxon	87,707	116,940	5,010	7,686	1,245,000	3.96	2.47
Ford	173,663	97,650	860	4,553	473,100	1.86	3.00
General Electric	153,884	58,414	4,303	16,997	873,120	4.85	1.88
Georgia-Pacific	12,060	12,665	365	5,218	86,704	4.28	1.60
IBM	87,568	69,018	6,020	11,949	571,391	10.51	4.84
Phillip Morris	46,569	51,169	3,540	15,285	926,219	3.83	1.46
Procter & Gamble	18,487	24,081	1,602	3,588	346,294	4.49	1.85
Sara Lee	7,636	11,606	470	1,524	230,339	1.91	.84

Appendix D
Public Announcement of Bond Issue

This announcement is neither an offer to sell nor a solicitation of offers to buy any of these securities. The offering is made only by the Prospectus and the related Prospectus Supplement.

<u>NEW ISSUE</u>   August 22, 1991

$250,000,000

Tenneco Credit Corporation

9⅝% Notes Due 2001

Price 99.566%

plus accrued interest from August 15, 1991

Copies of the Prospectus and the related Prospectus Supplement may be obtained in any State in which this announcement is circulated only from such of the undersigned as may legally offer these securities in such State.

The First Boston Corporation

J.P. Morgan Securities Inc.

Morgan Stanley & Co.
Incorporated

Appendix E
Bond Maturity and Interest Rate Risk

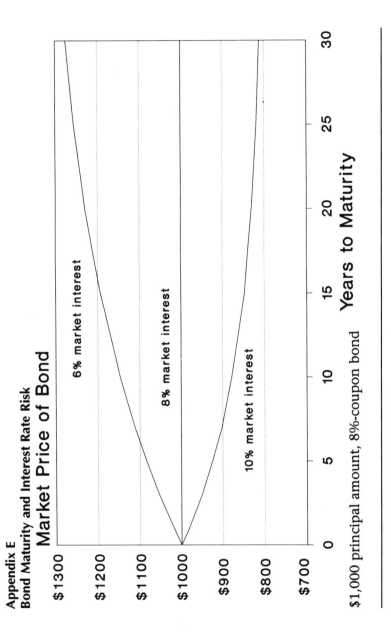

Market Price of Bond

6% market interest

8% market interest

10% market interest

$1300

$1200

$1100

$1000

$900

$800

$700

0   5   10   15   20   25   30

Years to Maturity

$1,000 principal amount, 8%-coupon bond

Appendix F
Treasury Bond Yield Curve

Annual Yield

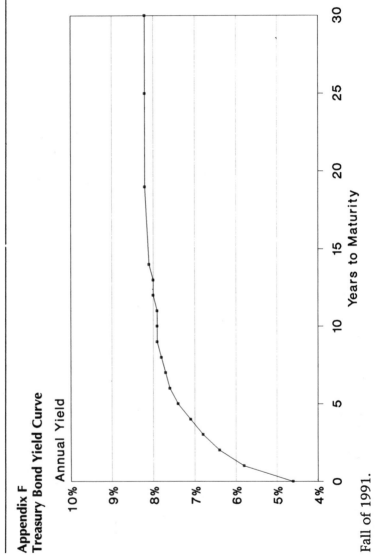

Fall of 1991.

Appendix G
Corporate and Municipal Bond Ratings

Moody's	S&P	
Aaa	AAA	High-grade with extremely strong capacity to pay principal and interest.
Aa	AA	High-grade by all standards but with slightly lower margins of protection than AAA.
A	A	Medium-grade with favorable investment attributes but with some susceptibility to adverse economic changes.
Baa	BBB	Medium-grade with adequate capacity to pay interest and principal but possibly lacking certain protection against adverse economic conditions.
Ba	BB	Speculative with moderate protection of principal and interest in an unstable economy.
B	B	Speculative and lacking desirable characteristics of investment bonds. Small assurance of principal and interest.
Caa	CCC	Issue in default or in danger of default.
Ca	CC	Highly speculative and in default or with other market shortcomings.
C	C	Extremely poor investment quality.
	C	Income bonds paying no interest.
	D	In default with interest or principal in arrears.

Appendix H
How Stocks Have Performed NYSE Composite Index, 1950–1990

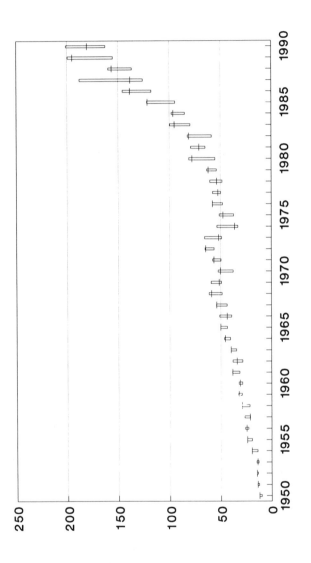

Appendix I
Measures of Stock Market Performance

Although investors typically think of the Dow Jones Industrial Average ("the Dow") when they inquire how the stock market has performed, there are actually numerous measures of stock market performance. Among these are:

Dow Jones Industrial Average—A price-weighted average of the stocks of 30 large industrial companies. The sum of the prices of the 30 stocks is divided a factor that is continually adjusted to take account of stock splits and changes in the composition of the average. Higher-priced stocks have a proportionally influence on the average. Some market watchers consider the Dow to be too narrow and too biased toward blue chip stocks to provide an accurate representation of the overall market.

Standard & Poor's 500 Composite Index—A measure based upon the market values (share price times the number of outstanding shares) of 500 stocks that include 400 industrials, 40 utilities, 20 transportation, and 40 financial firms. The S&P 500 includes some over-the-counter stocks and is calculated using a base of ten in the years 1941-1943. Standard & Poor's also publishes indexes for specialized stock series.

New York Stock Exchange Composite Index—A value-weighted index that includes all stocks listed on the New York Stock Exchange although the index is heavily influenced by the stocks of large corporations. The Exchange also provides separate indexes for industrial, utility, transportation, and financial stocks.

American Stock Exchange Market Value Index—A value-weighted index that includes stocks, American Depositary Receipts, and warrants listed on the American Stock Exchange.

NASDAQ Series—A value-weighted price indicator series that includes thousands of stocks traded in the over-the-counter market. Seven separate series are calculated for industrials, banks, insurance, other financial firms, transportation, utilities, and a composite measure that incorporates all of the stocks included in the other series. The NASDAQ Series is calculated using February 5, 1971, as a base of 100.

Wilshire 5000 Equity Index—A value-weighted index for 5000 common stocks including all NYSE and AMEX issues plus active over-the-counter stocks. The Wilshire Index is calculated using 1980 as the base year.

Value Line Averages—An index of the prices of approximately 1700 stocks reviewed by Value Line. Each of the stocks is equally weighted (neither price or market value makes one stock more important than any other stock) and the index is calculated with a base of 100 in 1961.

Appendix J
Most Active Stocks on the New York Stock Exchange, 1990

Stock		**Reported Volume**
1)	Philip Morris	448,780,400
2)	American Telephone & Telegraph	358,179,700
3)	International Business Machines	341,426,800
4)	General Electric	325,881,200
5)	Citicorp	323,847,700
6)	Federal National Mortgage	282,286,900
7)	American Express	274,643,100
8)	Exxon	246,706,800
9)	General Motors	243,767,300
10)	Boeing	234,405,000
11)	Wal-Mart Stores	227,087,600
12)	Waste Management	221,898,000
13)	Bristol-Myers Squibb	218,107,600
14)	Eastman Kodak	208,754,000
15)	Chase Manhattan	204,899,600

Appendix K
New York Stock Exchange Average Daily Share Volume, 1960–1990

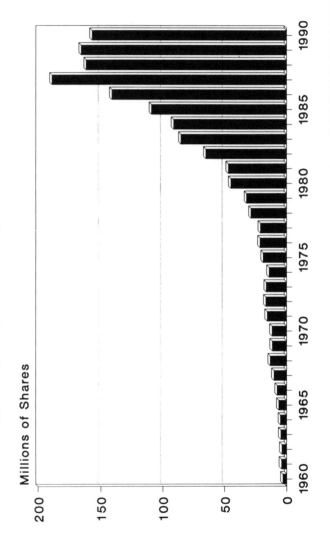

Millions of Shares

Appendix L
Prices of Membership on the New York Stock Exchange

Year	Low Price	High Price
1950	$ 46,000	$ 54,000
1955	80,000	90,000
1960	135,000	162,000
1965	190,000	250,000
1970	130,000	320,000
1971	145,000	300,000
1972	150,000	250,000
1973	72,000	190,000
1974	65,000	105,000
1975	55,000	138,000
1976	40,000	104,000
1977	35,000	95,000
1978	46,000	105,000
1979	82,000	210,000
1980	175,000	275,000
1981	220,000	285,000
1982	190,000	340,000
1983	310,000	425,000
1984	290,000	400,000
1985	310,000	425,000
1986	455,000	600,000
1987	605,000	1,150,000
1988	580,000	820,000
1989	420,000	675,000
1990	250,000	430,000

Source: New York Stock Exchange, *Fact Book 1991*.

Appendix M
Selected List of Discount Brokers

Brown & Co. Securities Corp.
Boston, MA
800-225-6707

Fidelity Brokerage Services, Inc.
Boston, MA
800-544-7272

Andrew Peck Associates, Inc.
New York, NY
800-221-5873

Quick & Reilly, Inc.
New York, NY
800-221-5220

Charles Schwab & Co., Inc.
San Francisco, CA
800-648-5300

Muriel Siebert & Co., Inc.
New York, NY
800-872-0711

Waterhouse Securities, Inc.
New York, NY
800-765-5185

Appendix N
Initial Margin Requirement to Purchase Stock, 1960–1990

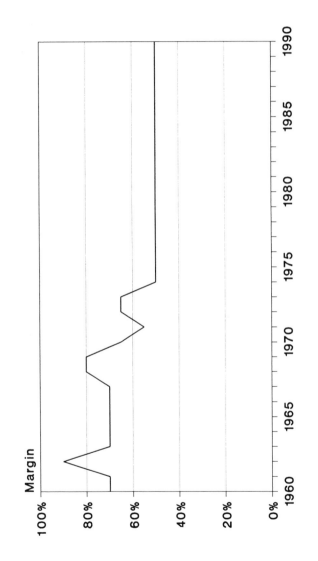

Appendix O
Comprehensive Asset Management Accounts

A comprehensive brokerage account termed the *Cash Management Account (CMA)* was introduced by Merrill Lynch in the late 1970s. The CMA account was soon imitated by a number of other brokerage firms and what is referred to generically as the *asset management account* gained substantial popularity during the 1980s. The limited number of brokerage firms that offer this type account do so under various trademarked names, but the accounts have similar features that generally include:

1) Automatic daily or weekly sweeps of any cash in the account into a money market fund sponsored by the brokerage firm. Some firms provide a daily sweep of funds while other firms sweep weekly unless an especially large amount of cash is involved. Most firms provide investors with a choice of several money market funds including a regular fund, a tax-exempt fund, and a fund that invests only in U.S. government securities.

2) Unlimited check writing privileges against money market fund balances. Funds in the account earn interest until checks are presented for payment at which time shares in the fund are sold.

3) Automatic investment of dividends and interest from securities kept in the account, and proceeds from any securities sales into the money market fund.

4) A comprehensive monthly account statement and an end-of-year statement of itemized income items for tax-reporting.

5) A debit or credit card with purchase amounts from card use deducted from the account's money market fund. Shares in the money market fund are sold to produce a cash balance that is used to pay the charge. Most firms provide a debit card (money market fund shares are sold immediately when the purchase amount is presented for payment) as part of the account and offer a credit card (shares in the money market fund are sold to pay for card purchases at the end of the statement period) at an additional annual fee of $25 to $35.

6) Account insurance beyond the $500,000 provided by the Securities Investor Protection Corporation.

7) Margin borrowing using as collateral securities kept in the account. Checks and credit card purchases can amount to more than an account's money market balance.

Brokerage firms that offer asset management accounts generally require that an investor make an initial deposit of from $5,000 to $20,000 (the amount depending upon the brokerage firm) in either cash or securities to open an account. The firms generally levy an annual charge that ranges from $60 to $100. Some of the firms that offer asset management accounts are:

Dean Witter—The firm's Active Assets Account requires a minimum initial deposit of $10,000 in cash or securities. The account costs $80 annually and includes a Visa credit card at no additional charge.

Fidelity Brokerage Services—The Ultra Service Account requires a $25,000 deposit of cash or securities. Fidelity charges $5 per month for the account and an optional Gold MasterCard or Visa Gold card is an additional $24 annually.

Merrill Lynch—The Cash Management Account requires an initial deposit of $20,000 in cash or securities. With a Visa debit card the annual fee is $100. There is an additional charge for a credit card.

Charles Schwab and Company—The Schwab One Account requires an initial deposit of $5,000 in cash or securities. No annual fee is charged.

Shearson Lehman Brothers—The Financial Management Account requires an initial deposit of $20,000 in cash or securities. With an American Express Gold Card, the annual account fee is $100. Investors with substantial assets can obtain the account without paying an annual fee.

Appendix P
Stocks Used in Calculating the Dow Jones Averages

Dow Jones Industrial Average (30 stocks)

Allied-Signal
Aluminum Company of America
American Express
American Telephone and Telegraph
Bethlehem Steel
Boeing
Caterpillar
Chevron
Coca-Cola
Disney
Du Pont
Eastman Kodak
Exxon
General Electric
General Motors
Goodyear
International Business Machines
International Paper
McDonalds
Merck
Minnesota Mining & Manufacturing
Morgan (J.P.)
Philip Morris
Procter & Gamble
Sears
Texaco
Union Carbide
United Technology
Westinghouse
Woolworth

Dow Jones Transportation Average (20 stocks)

AMR
Airborne Freight
Alaska Air Group
American President Companies
Burlington Northern
Carolina Freight
Consolidated Freight
Consolidated Rail
CSX
Delta Airlines
Federal Express
Norfolk Southern
Roadway Services
Ryder System
Santa Fe Pacific
Southwest Airlines
UAL
Union Pacific
USAir Group
Xtra

Dow Jones Utility Average (15 stocks)

American Electric Power
Arkla
Centerior Energy
Commonwealth Edison
Consolidated Edison
Consolidated Natural Gas
Detroit Edison
Houston Industries
Niagra Mohawk
Pacific Gas & Electric
Panhandle Eastern

Peoples Energy
Philadelphia Electric
Public Service Enterprise Group
SCECorp

Appendix Q
Interpreting Stock and Bond Quotations

Stock Quotations

52 Weeks					Yld		Vol				Net
Hi	Lo	Stock	Sym	Div	%	PE	100s	Hi	Lo	Close	Chg
11 5/8	5	GenCorp	GY	.60	5.5	8	180	11 1/8	11	11	- 1/4

52-week high and low: The highest price and lowest price attained by this stock during the preceding 52 weeks. Stocks are traded in eighths of a dollar per share. An eighth is 12 1/2 cents. GenCorp reached a high price of $11.625 per share and a low price of $5 per share during the preceding 52 weeks.

Stock: The abbreviated name of the stock. Names are sometimes abbreviated to the point that it is difficult to determine what the abbreviation represents.

Symbol: The ticker symbol for this stock. This series of letters appears in boardrooms when a trade in the stock occurs and is generally the coding to obtain the stock's price on a quotation machine.

Dividend: The current annual dividend per share. GenCorp is paying an annual cash dividend of $0.60 per share. The owner of 100 shares of this stock will receive a $15 check every three months.

Yield in percent: The current dividend yield that is calculated by dividing the indicated dividend by the closing price. GenCorp's dividend yield is $0.60/$11, or 5.5 percent. The yield changes with changes in the dividend and changes in the price of the stock. The stated yield does not consider any potential increases or decreases in the price of the stock.

PE: The price-earnings ratio (PE or P/E ratio) is calculated by dividing the closing stock price by the earnings per share. The P/E ratio indicates the number of dollars an investor must pay to purchase a dollar of the firm's current earnings. The P/E ratio can be a useful investment statistic but it sometimes severely impacted by temporary aberrations in reported earnings.

Volume: The amount of round lot trading in the stock during the day's activity. Total round lot volume is 100 times the number listed in the volume column.

Hi: The highest price at which GenCorp stock traded during the session.

Lo: The lowest price at which GenCorp stock traded during the session.

Close: The last price at which GenCorp stock traded during the session. During this session GenCorp closed at $11 per share, the stock's lowest price of the day.

Net change: The difference between GenCorp's closing price this session and GenCorp's closing price during the session in which the stock last traded. The net change of 1/4 ($0.25 per share) indicates that the $11 closing price is $0.25 per share less than the previous day's closing price of $11.25. Thus, GenCorp stock closed down $0.25 per share.

Bond Quotations

Bonds	Cur Yld	Vol	Close	Net Chg
Amoco 8 3/8s05	8.4	247	99 3/4	− 3/8

Bonds: The issuer of the bond and the bond's coupon and year of maturity. The Amoco bond has an 8.375 percent coupon rate (annually pays 8.375 percent of the bond's $1,000 face value). The bond is scheduled to mature sometime in 2005 (the exact date is available in other publications) although there is a possibility the bond is callable at an earlier date.

Current yield: The bond's yield from interest payments only. Current yield is calculated by dividing the bond's annual interest income ($837.50) by the closing price. Potential changes in the bond's market price are not included in the calculation of current yield.

Close: The last price at which the bond traded during the session. Bonds are quoted in percent of par value. The Amoco bond had a closing price of 99.75 percent of $1,000, or $997.50.

Net change: The amount by which the bond's closing price this trading session is different than the bond's closing price at the previous session during which the security traded. The 3/8 decline means that each Amoco bond lost .3875 times $1,000, or $38.75 in value. Because bonds frequently don't trade for days at a time the previous closing price may have occured many days or weeks in the past.

Appendix R
Selected List of Large Mutual Fund Distributors

Colonial Investment Services
One Financial Center
Boston, MA 02111
800-225-2365

Dreyfus Service Corporation
144 Glenn Curtiss Boulevard
Uniondale, NY 11556
800-782-6620

Fidelity Distributors Corporation
82 Devonshire Street
Boston, MA 02109
800-544-6666

Franklin Distributors
777 Maariner's Island Boulevard
6th Floor
San Mateo, CA 94404

IDS Financial Services
IDS Tower 10
Minneapolis, MN 55440
800-328-8300

Kemper Financial Services
120 South LaSalle Street
Chicago, IL 60603
800-621-1048

Massachusetts Financial Services
PO Box 2281
Boston, MA 02107
800-225-2606

T Rowe Price Associates
100 East Pratt Street
Baltimore, MD 21202
800-638-5660

Putnam Financial Services
PO Box 2701
Boston, MA 02208
800-225-1581

Scudder Fund Distributors
160 Federal Street
Boston, MA 02110
800-225-2470

USAA Investment Management
USAA Building
San Antonio, TX 78284
800-531-8181

Value Line Securities
711 Third Avenue
New York, NY 10017
800-223-0818

Vanguard Group of Investment Companies
PO Box 2600
MS 136
Valley Forge, PA 19482
800-662-7447

Appendix S
Mutual Fund Sales and Redemptions, 1970–1990

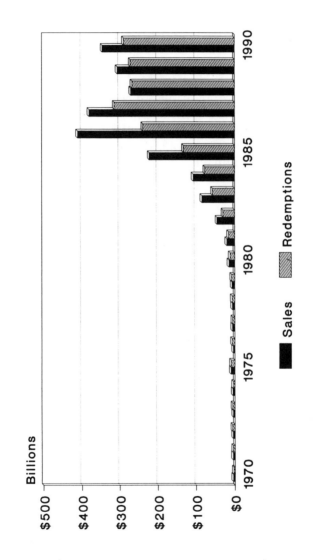

Billions

Appendix T
Comparing Taxable and Tax-Free Yields

To determine if municipal bonds or tax-exempt mutual funds are appropriate investments, investors must be able to compare the returns from these investments with the after-tax returns that are available from alternative investments. For example, the return from a high-grade municipal bond with twenty years to maturity should be compared to the after-tax return from a high-grade corporate bond or to a Treasury bond of similar maturity.

To calculate the after-tax return from a taxable investment multiply the taxable investment's anticipated return by one minus your effective federal tax rate. If you pay federal taxes on the highest portion of your income (termed your *marginal tax rate*) at a rate of 28 percent, subtract 0.28 from 1.0 and multiply the difference, 0.72, times the return that you can earn on the taxable investment. If the resulting after-tax return on the taxable investment is greater than the return on an equivalent municipal bond the taxable investment will provide the higher after-tax return.

After-tax return = TR × (1 − MTR)
where:

> TR is the taxable return available from an investment
> MTR is an investor's marginal income tax rate

To calculate the taxable return that is equivalent to the return offered by a tax-exempt investment ("What return would I require on a taxable investment to equal the return that is provided by this tax-exempt investment?") divide the tax-exempt return by one minus your effective federal tax rate. Suppose a tax-exempt money market fund offers an annual return of five percent. To calculate the equivalent taxable return, divide 5 percent by 1 minus 0.28, or 0.72, and obtain 6.94 percent. Thus, if you can earn more than 6.94 percent on a taxable money market fund at the same time that a tax-exempt fund is yielding five percent, you should choose the taxable fund because the taxable fund provides you with a greater after-tax return.

Equivalent taxable return = TFR/(1 − MTR)
where:

> TFR is the tax-free return from an investment
> MTR is the investor's marginal income tax rate

The fact that Treasury securities and some municipal securities are also exempt from state and local taxes complicates the analysis somewhat and can tip the balance to favor these securities when the comparison with yields on taxable investments is a close one. Also, a higher personal federal income tax rate makes it more likely that tax-exempt securities are a superior choice of investments.

Appendix U
Taxable and Tax-Exempt Interest Rates 1950–1990

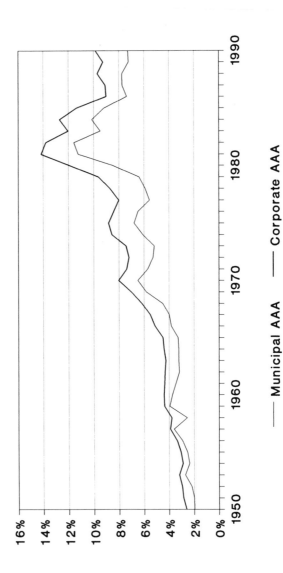

Appendix V
Federal Income Tax Rates, 1991

Taxpayers filing a joint return

Taxable Income	Tax Rate
$ 0 to $32,450	15%
32,451 to 78,400	28%
all over 78,401	31%

Taxpayers filing a single return

Taxable Income	Tax Rate
$ 0 to $17,450	15%
19,451 to 47,050	28%
all over 47,050	31%

Suppose you and your spouse together earned $70,000 in 1991. After all adjustments, deductions, and exemptions this gross income resulted in a taxable income of $50,000. Your tax (using the joint return table) would be calculated as 15 percent of the first $32,450 plus 28 percent of the $17,550 difference between $32,450 and your taxable income of $50,000. The result is a tax liability of $4,867.50 + $4,914.00, or $9,781.50. A single individual with the same taxable income would have a tax liability of (0.15 × $17,450) + (0.28 × $29,600) + (0.31 × $2,950), or $11,820.

Appendix W
Annual Inflation, 1965–1990

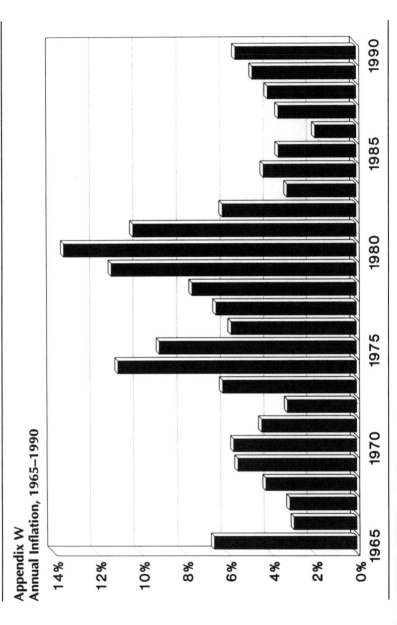

Appendix X
Purchasing Power of the Dollar, 1950–1990

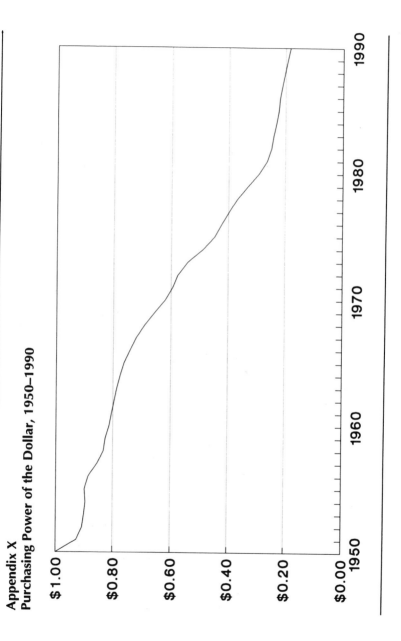

Appendix Y
Important Dividend Dates for Stockholders

A firm's directors normally meet to conduct the company's business four times per year. One of the important issues discussed at the meetings relates to the dividend that will be paid to stockholders. Directors must decide if any dividend is to be paid and, if so, what size the dividend will be, and when the payment will occur. Also, directors must decide upon the date that will be used to determine which stockholders will receive the dividend.

Four important dates relate to cash dividends:

1) Declaration date—The day directors convene and decide upon the dividend. The directors announce the size of the dividend, the date that stockholders must be recorded as owners in order to be entitled to the dividend, and the date the dividend will be paid.

2) Ex-dividend date—The first day that new buyers of the company's stock will not be entitled to the dividend that directors have declared. Investors who purchase the firm's stock on or after the ex-dividend date will not receive the dividend that was declared at the last directors' meeting.

3) Record date—The day the firm closes its corporate register of security owners in determining who is to receive the announced dividend. The ex-dividend date precedes the record date by four business days. The four-day difference results from investors having five business days to pay for stock that has been purchased.

4) Payment date—The day the firm or the firm's agent makes the dividend payment to individuals who appear on the record date as stockholders.

As an illustration of the dividend sequence, suppose a firm's directors convene on September 3 and determine that a dividend of $0.30 per share will be paid to stockholders of record on September 20, with payments to be mailed October 1. Examining the September calendar we see that investors who have purchased the stock by the close of business on September 13 (Friday) will receive the dividend to be paid on September 30. Someone who purchases the firm's shares on September 16 (Monday, the ex-dividend date) will not receive the dividend to be paid on September 30. No dividend will be received by a September 16 buyer because that buyer will not have to pay for the stock until five business days (September 23) following the date of purchase. Thus, ownership of the stock will not be transferred until September 23, one business day beyond the required record date.

Sun	Mon	Tues	Wed	Thur	Fri	Sat
1	2	3	4	5	6	7
8	9	10	11	12	13	14
15	16	17	18	19	20	21
22	23	24	25	26	27	28
29	30					

Appendix Z
Glossary

Account statement: A statement of investment activity and investment position that is periodically (generally monthly) sent by brokerage firms to their customers.

Active: Describing a security in which there is substantial trading.

Adjustment to conversion terms: A change in the terms by which a security may be exchanged.

After-hours trading: Trading in securities following the close of the organized exchanges.

After-tax return: The return on an investment after expected income taxes have been subtracted.

Aggressive investing: Investing in risky assets in an attempt to earn relatively high returns.

All-or-none order: An order to purchase or to sell a security in which the entire amount of the order must be traded.

Alternative minimum tax (ATM): A federal tax on taxable income as adjusted for certain specified deductions and income items.

American Depositary Receipt (ADR): A receipt on foreign securities that are being held in trust.

American Stock Exchange (AMEX): An organized securities exchange located in New York City that trades securities that have national interest.

Arbitrage: Simultaneously purchasing and selling different assets that are substantially the same to take advantage of price differences that exist between the assets.

Ask: The quoted price at which a security will be sold.

Asset: Something of value that is owned by an individual or by an organization.

Average: An aggregate measure of security prices.

Basis point: One-hundredth of one percent.

Bear: An investor who believes a certain stock or the entire stock market is headed for a decline.

Bear market: A long period of declining security prices.

Bid: The price being offered by a potential buyer for a security.

Big Board: The New York Stock Exchange.

Blue chip: A high-quality company or security.

Bond: A long-term promissory note.

Bond rating: A grading of a bond issuer's ability to meet scheduled interest and principal payments (See Appendix G).

Bottom: The lowest value to which the stock market or a particular stock will fall.

Broker: An individual or firm that acts as an intermediary between a buyer and a seller.

Bull: An investor who expects the price of a stock or of the general stock market to increase in value.

Bull market: A long period of rising security prices.

Buy-and-hold strategy: Holding securities for long periods in order to reduce transactions costs and avoid selling on temporary declines.

Buyback: A firm's repurchase of its own securities.

Call: 1. An option that permits a the owner of the call to purchase a certain asset at a specified price until a certain date. 2. The redemption of a bond prior to the bond's scheduled maturity.

Capital gain: The amount by which the proceeds from the sale of an asset exceed the asset's cost.

Capital gains tax: A tax on capital gains from assets that are sold.

Cash account: A brokerage account that requires cash payment for security purchases.

Certificate: Evidence of ownership of shares of stock or of a bond.

Close: The last price at which a security trades or the last valuation of a stock price average during a trading session.

Common stock: A class of stock that has no priority to dividends or to assets in the event of liquidation.

Composite tape: A security price reporting system that includes trading from all of the organized exchanges and from the over-the-counter market.

Confirmation: Written acknowledgment that a security order has been executed.

Conversion price: The price at which shares of common stock will be exchanged for a convertible security.

Convertible security: A security that can be exchanged for another asset.

Corporation: A business that has its own rights and obligations that are separate from the owners of the business.

Coupon: The annual rate of interest paid on a debt security as calculated on the basis of the security's face value.

Creditor: The person or organization to which a debt is owed.

Current asset: Cash or an asset that will be converted into cash within one year.

Current liability: A debt that is due to be paid within one year.

Current yield: The rate of return to be earned from an investment based upon the investment's expected annual cash payment and the investment's current market price.

Cyclical: The stock of a business with profits that are subject to substantial swings throughout a business cycle.

Day order: An order to buy or sell a security that will be automatically canceled at the end of trading on the day the order is entered.

Dealer: An individual or organization that purchases assets for and sells assets from its own portfolio.

Debenture: A corporate debt security that has no specific asset pledged as collateral.

Declaration date: The date when a firm's officers announce the amount and date of the firm's next stock dividend.

Defensive stock: A stock that tends to resist declines in the stock market.

Delivery: Transfer of a security to the seller's broker.

Discount brokerage firm: A brokerage firm that executes security trades for commissions that are less than those charged by most full-service brokers.

Diversification: The acquisition of various assets with returns that are not directly related.

Dividend: A payment from profits that is distributed to stockholders.

Dividend reinvestment plan: A corporate plan in which stockholders may elect to have the firm utilize dividend payments to purchase additional shares of stock.

Dollar-cost averaging: An investment plan in which an individual makes an equal dollar investment each period.

Dow Jones Industrial Average ("The Dow"): A trademark for one of the oldest and most widely quoted measures of stock market price movements.

Earnings per share (EPS): A corporation's net income after taxes divided by the number of shares of the firm's common stock that is outstanding.

Equity: 1. Stock, either common or preferred. 2. The market value of securities that are held in a brokerage account less the amount borrowed on the securities. 3. Funds in a business that have been contributed by owners.

Ex-dividend: Pertaining to a stock that no longer carries the right to the next dividend payment.

Ex-dividend date: The first date a buyer of stock will not receive the next dividend.

Federal agency security: The security of a federal agency such as the Government National Mortgage Association.

Fixed-income security: A security that makes a fixed periodic payment to the owner of the security.

Flat: Pertaining to a bond that is traded without accrued interest.

Full-service brokerage firm: A brokerage firm that provides customers with a wide range of products and services including advice concerning what securities to buy and sell.

Going public: The initial sale of stock to the public by a firm that has been privately held.

Good-till-canceled order: A order to buy or sell a security that remains in effect until executed or until canceled by the investor who placed the order.

Growth fund: An investment company with an investment objective of long-term capital growth.

Growth stock: The common stock of a company that is expected to have above-average growth in revenues and profits.

High-grade: Pertaining to the security of an issuer with good credit quality.

Inactive security: A security that seldom trades or that trades in small amounts.

Index fund: A mutual fund that maintains a portfolio of stocks so as to match the performance of the entire market.

Initial public offering (IPO): A corporation's first public offering of common stock.

Institutional investor: An organization such as a bank trust department or an insurance company that invests substantial amounts of money.

Investment banker: A firm that provides assistance to organizations who are in need of raising outside funds.

Investment company: A firm that pools and then reinvests funds that have been invested by individuals.

Issue: 1. A particular class of an organization's securities. 2. To sell securities in the primary market.

Joint account agreement: A form that places a brokerage account in the names of two or more individuals.

Joint ownership: Ownership by two or more parties.

Junk bond: A bond with a low credit rating (or, no credit rating) in which there is considerable doubt that the terms of the bond will be satisfied.

Leveraged buyout (LBO): Using a firm's assets as collateral for loans that finance the purchase of the firm.

Limit order: A investor's order to execute a security trade only at a specified price or better.

Limit price: The price specified on a limit order.

Liquidity: The degree to which there is a large amount of cash or of assets that are readily convertible to cash.

Listed security: A security that has been admitted to trading on one of the organized securities exchanges.

Load: The fee that investors are charged when they acquire shares of an investment company.

Low-load fund: A mutual fund with a relatively low sales fee that ranges from one to three percent of the amount invested.

Maintenance fee: The annual fee charged to customers by some brokerage firms to maintain a brokerage account.

Major turn: A reversal in the intermediate- or long-term direction of the stock market's movement.

Managed account: A brokerage account that is managed by a broker or by a professional investment adviser.

Management fee: The annual fee charged to investors who own shares of an investment company.

Margin: The amount of unencumbered value that must be deposited in order to purchase or to maintain a security position.

Margin account: A brokerage account that permits an investor to buy securities on credit or to borrow against securities that are already deposited in the account.

Market order: An investor's order to immediately execute a security trade at the best possible price.

Market price: The price at which a security trades in the secondary market.

Market timing: Frequent trading of securities in order to take advantage of short-term price movements.

Maturity: The date on which a financial obligation is to be paid.

Maturity value: The amount to be paid to the owner of a security at the security's maturity.

Momentum: The tendency of the market or of a security to continue moving in the same direction.

Money market: The market for short-term securities such as negotiable certificates of deposit and Treasury bills.

Money market fund: A mutual fund that purchases short-term, high-quality securities and passes through interest received from these securities to the fund's shareholders.

Most-active list: The listing of securities that have exhibited the greatest volume of trading during a certain period of time.

Municipal bond: A debt security issued by a state, city, county, or some other political subdivision. Most municipal bonds pay interest that is exempt from taxation by the federal government.

Mutual fund: An investment company that continually stands ready to sell new shares of its own stock and to redeem existing shares of its own stock.

Negotiable: Pertaining to a financial instrument for which ownership can be easily transferred.

Net change: The amount by which a security's closing price is different from the closing price in the previous trading period.

Net proceeds: The amount of funds (pretax) that are actually received from the sale of an asset.

Net worth: The value of all assets less the amount of money that is owed on the assets.

New issue: A security that is being offered to the public for the first time.

New York Stock Exchange (NYSE): The oldest and largest organized securities exchange in the United States.

No-load fund: A mutual fund that is sold without a sales charge.

Odd lot: A quantity of securities that is less than the standard trading unit. Less than 100 shares of a common stock are considered an odd lot.

On the sidelines: Describing an investor who has decided to wait before committing funds for investment.

Opening: The beginning of a securities trading session.

Option: A contract that allows the owner to either purchase or sell (depending upon the type of option) an asset at a specified price until a certain date.

Option writer: The investor who originates an option.

Original maturity: The time between when a bond is issued and when the bond is scheduled for maturity.

Overbought: Pertaining to a stock market that has recently experienced a significant rise and that is likely to experience declines in the near future.

Oversold: Pertaining to a stock market that has recently experienced a significant decline and that is likely to experience increases in the near future.

Over-the-counter market (OTC): The linking of dealers that make markets in many securities.

Partial execution: Execution of less than the full amount of an order.

Par value: A security's stated value as printed on the certificate.

Payment date: The date on which a dividend or interest will be paid to a security's owner.

Payout ratio: The proportion of net income that a firm pays out in cash dividends.

Penny stock: A low-priced stock whose ownership generally entails substantial risk.

Point: A measure of change in the value of a security or of a market average.

Portfolio: A group of investments.

Post: The location on the floor of an organized securities exchange at which a particular stock is traded.

Preemptive right: The right of a stockholder to maintain proportional ownership of a firm by acquiring a portion of new shares that are being sold to the public.

Preferred stock: Shares of business ownership that give the owner of the stock priority (over common stockholders) with respect to dividends and to assets in the event of a liquidation.

Price-earnings ratio (PE or P/E ratio): The   current market value of a stock divided by the firm's earnings per share.

Principal: A bond's face amount.

Profit taking: Widespread selling of a stock or of securities in general following an extended rise in value.

Prospectus: A formal document containing relevant facts concerning an issue of securities.

Proxy: Written authorization to act for a stockholder.

Publicly traded company: A business with shares of ownership that are traded on an organized exchange or in the over-the-counter market and that are available for purchase.

Put: An option that gives the owner the right to sell a particular asset at a specified price until a given date.

Quotation: A listing or statement of the value of a security.

Range: The high price and low price at which a security or a market average has attained during a given period.

Rating: The grading of the credit quality of a debt obligation.

Rating Agencies: Companies that grade the credit quality of debt obligations.

Record date: The date on which an organization determines who holds securities for the purpose of paying dividends, sending financial statements, and so forth.

Redemption: The retirement of a security by the security's issuer.

Regional exchange: An organized securities exchange that specializes in the securities of companies located in the region of the exchange.

Registered representative: A brokerage firm employee who is registered with the Securities and Exchange commission to handle investor accounts.

Registration: The preparation of a securities issue for public sale.

Registration statement: A formal document filed with the Securities and Exchange Commission by an organization planning to publicly issue securities.

Rights offering: The distribution to existing stockholders of rights to purchase shares that are part of a new common stock issue.

Round lot: The standard unit of trading for a particular type of security.

Secondary market: The market in which outstanding securities are traded.

Secondary stock: The common stock of a smaller company that is not generally an industry leader.

Sector fund: An investment company that concentrates on investing in securities having a commonality. For example, a sector fund may buy only the stocks of energy companies.

Securities Investor Protection Corporation (SIPC): A government-sponsored organization that insures cash and securities held in brokerage accounts.

Short sale: The sale of a security that is not owned and must be borrowed.

Size: The number of bonds or shares of stock that are being offered for sale or bid for at the quoted price.

Specialist: A member of an organized securities exchange who makes a market in one or more securities.

Speculator: An individual who is willing to take large risks in order to earn above-average returns. Speculators generally hold securities for a relatively short period of time.

Split: An increase in the number of shares of stock outstanding without an accompanying increase in assets.

Standard & Poor's 500 Stock Index: A comprehensive stock index that is calculated using the market values of the common stocks of 500 companies.

Stock: Shares of ownership in a corporation.

Stock dividend: A dividend that is comprised of additional shares of stock to a corporation's owners.

Street name: Registration of an investor's security in the name of the brokerage firm that is holding the security.

SuperDOT: A New York Stock Exchange system that automatically routes customer orders to the appropriate specialist.

Swap: To exchange one asset for another.

Tax-loss selling: Selling securities in order to realize a loss in value for tax purposes.

Technical rally: A short-term rise in the stock market that is an interruption to a longer-term decline.

Tender offer: An offer to purchase stock from investors.

Top: The highest value to which the stock market or a particular stock will rise.

Total return: A security's yield to investors that includes both current income and changes in market value.

Trader: A person who buys and sells securities in an attempt to profit from short-term changes in value.

Treasury bill: A short-term (one year or less) debt security issued and guaranteed by the U.S. Treasury.

Unlisted: Describing a security that trades in the over-the- counter market and has not been approved for trading on an organized securities exchange.

Uptrend: A series of increases in value for a specific stock or for the overall market.

Value investing: The purchase of securities based upon the market value of assets that are owned by the firms that have issued the securities.

Volume: Units of trading in a security or in the overall market for a specified period.

Voting stock: Stock that gives the owner of the stock the right to vote for the firm's directors.

Warrant: A security that allows an investor to purchase a specific number of shares of stock at a predetermined price.

When-issued: Pertaining to a security that has not yet been issued.

Yield: The rate of return to be earned on an investment.

Yield to maturity: The annual rate of return to be earned from buying a debt security at the current market price when the security will be held until the scheduled maturity.

Zero-coupon bond: A bond that is issued at a large discount from face value and that makes no periodic interest payments.

INDEX

A

Active stocks, 162
ADRs, *see* American
    Depository Receipts
After-tax return, 129
American Depository
    Receipts, 72
American Stock Exchange,
    6, 91-92, 98, 100
American Telephone and
    Telegraph, 18, 19, 42,
    75
Amoco, 19
Appendices, 152-202
Apple Computer, 42, 72
Appreciation
    taxes, 130
Ask, 75
Asked (price), 45
Asset, 28, 57
AT&T, *see* American
    Telephone and
    Telegraph

Average daily share
    volume (NYSE), 163

B

Balanced funds, 117
Balance sheet, 106
Bankruptcy, 35
Barron's, 80, 91, 96
Bid, 45, 75
Black and Decker, 2
Blue chip stock, 19
Board of directors, 24-25
Bond
    see corporate and
    municipal bond ratings
    characteristics, 27-40
    definition, 2, 27-28
    denominations, 29-30
    interest, 33-34
    liquidation, 35
    maturity, 156
    origination, 28
    quotations, 99

ABOUT THE AUTHOR

David L. Scott is Professor of Accounting and Finance at Valdosta State College, Valdosta, Georgia. He earned a B.S. at Purdue University, a M.S. at Florida State University, and a Ph.D. in Economics at the University of Arkansas at Fayetteville.

How Wall Street Works: The Basics and Beyond is the sixteenth book authored by Dr. Scott. He has published numerous articles and presented seminars on various investment topics. Previous books include *Understanding and Managing Investment Risk and Return* (Probus 1990) and *Investing in Tax-Saving Municipal Bonds* (Probus 1991). He also authored the reference guide, *Wall Street Words*, Houghton Mifflin.

Exceptional Titles from the Investor's Quick Reference Series

Mutual Funds Explained: The Basics & Beyond,
Robert C. Upton Jr., $14.95

Wall Street Words: The Basics & Beyond,
Richard J. Maturi, $14.95

Financial Statement Analysis: The Basics & Beyond,
Rose Marie L. Bukics, $14.95

*Managing Your Investments, Savings and Credit: The Basics
& Beyond*, $14.95, Esmé E. Faerber

Forthcoming Titles . . .

Municipal Bonds: The Basics & Beyond,
David L. Scott, $14.95, Available in March 1992

Please use order form on next page

ORDER FORM

Quantity	Title	Price

Payment: MasterCard/Visa/American Express accepted. When ordering by credit card your account will not be billed until the book is shipped. You may also reserve your order by phone or by mailing this order form. When ordering by check or money order, you will be invoiced upon publication. Upon receipt of your payment, the book will be shipped. Please add $3.50 for postage and handling for the first book and $1.00 for each additional copy.

Subtotal _____

IL residents add 7% tax _____

Shipping and Handling _____

Total _____

Credit Card # _____

Expiration Date _____

Name _____

Address _____

City, State, Zip _____

Telephone _____

Signature _____

Mail Orders to:

IRWIN PROFESSIONAL PUBLISHING
1333 Burr Ridge Parkway
Burr Ridge, IL 60521

1-800-634-3966

B11